# BADGE *of* HONOR

## Blowing the Whistle

*The True Story of a Mayor's Bodyguard*

## Walter L. Harris, Jr.

**Wasteland Press**
www.wastelandpresss.net
Shelbyville, KY USA

*Badge of Honor: Blowing the Whistle*
*The True Story of a Mayor's Bodyguard*
by Walter L. Harris, Jr.

First Printing – April 2011
ISBN: 978-1-60047-560-3

The following is a true story based on and inspired by true
events. Certain names and places have been changed to protect
the privacy of those mentioned. However, the main characters
of this story have appeared in local, state, and national news;
thus they are subject to public disclosure. *–WLHJr.*

Printed in the U.S.A.

0    1    2    3    4

*To my sons and daughter, may they remember the integrity of their father and the sacrifices he made in order to stand up for justice. That they may walk through life with honor, dignity, integrity, and faith in God.*

*To the men and women in blue, may you always honor your badge and boldly stand for justice without fearing the consequences.*

# Acknowledgments

The author gratefully acknowledges all advocates for truth who are still fighting and who will continue to fight for truth and justice. I would like to thank my wonderful, God-fearing mother who taught me always to do the right thing in any given situation. I am especially thankful to my soul mate and loving wife of 21 years, who supported me throughout the whistleblower ordeal and the writing of this book. In addition, I am grateful to my attorney, Michael Stefani, for his vigorous fight against the injustice I faced. I am equally grateful to my editor, Susan Giffin, an award-winning author and editor. After interviewing various editors, I knew she was the one whom I could trust to help me tell my story. Finally, I would be remiss if I did not thank my Detroit pastor who provided me guidance at the onset of the whistleblower ordeal.

# Contents

2001 Detroit Police Department Executive Protection Unit:
Harris (far right) is pictured with officers of his assigned crew,
along with former Mayor W. Dennis Archer and his wife, Trudy.

# Foreword

I was in my second term as mayor of the City of Detroit when Detroit Police Officer Walter L. Harris, Jr. walked into my office for an interview to join the Executive Protection Unit (EPU). The sergeant in charge of the unit had already completed a thorough background check of Officer Harris.

During my first term, the EPU earned tremendous respect from the FBI and the Secret Service, as well as the Michigan State Police, county and local city police departments, for the way they conducted themselves in providing security for me and my family. They also demonstrated professional excellence in working with the other law enforcement agencies when President Bill Clinton, Vice President Al Gore, members of President Clinton's cabinet, the Governor of Michigan or other dignitaries would visit Detroit. The Secret Service and the FBI provided training to the EPU because of the number of visits President Clinton's administration made to Detroit.

But there was more. Whenever I left Detroit on city business and met with other mayors who had police officer protection, Detroit's EPU seemed to stand out with class. There developed by and between the various city police departments a mutual respect for the manner in which the Detroit EPU conducted themselves.

There was an enormous amount of hard earned pride that developed after the EPU was the first organized under my administration on January 1, 1994. Therefore, as time passed by the sergeant in charge of the EPU was meticulous in the background check. It was absolutely imperative that a new officer assigned to the unit have a great track record within the police department, have an impeccable reputation for high integrity and high moral character, and could run at least 1½ miles at a reasonably fast pace of a seven minute mile.

Following my interview with Detroit Police Officer Walter L. Harris, Jr., I invited him to join the EPU. During Officer Harris' service until I left office at midnight, December 31, 2001, he was conscientious, principled, hard working, reliable, thorough, timely, a team player with his fellow officers and took great care of me and my family. He always demonstrated outstanding integrity and character during his service on my Executive Protection Unit.

Dennis W. Archer
Former Mayor of the City of Detroit
(1994-2001)
Chairman & CEO, Dennis W. Archer PLLC
Chair, Infilaw National Policy Board
Past President, American Bar Association
Chairman Emeritus, Dickinson Wright PLLC

# Introduction

*"For it is not easy to do the correct thing*
*when the people around you are*
*prospering from doing the wrong thing."*
*Walter L. Harris, Jr.*

During my career with the Detroit Police Department, I worked with many honorable police officers in precincts and in an assortment of specialized units. Unfortunately, my last year in the department was whittled by a seemingly insurmountable onslaught of dishonorable activities by officers in my unit. While assigned to the Detroit Police Executive Protection Unit (EPU) under Mayor Kwame Kilpatrick, I witnessed corruption and immoral activities. When I became a police officer, I promised myself that I would never dishonor my badge or compromise my integrity. Yet, I was soon expected to participate in various forms of corruption and immoral acts while on duty. Within 16 months of accepting my position in EPU with Mayor Kilpatrick, I voluntarily transferred out of what some would consider a prestigious unit. I needed to maintain my honor and avoid being implicated in the improper activities that were occurring regularly within this unit.

Since leaving Detroit, I have learned of the plight of two Detroit police officers who succumbed to the temptations of corruption. One dishonored his badge by receiving income from criminal activities and was sentenced to prison for tax evasion. The second officer dishonored his badge and was sent to federal prison for receiving a bribe in order to help facilitate the sale of city-owned property. In each case, these officers made decisions under the cover of the badge that they will regret for the rest of their lives. I look back on my situation and how I avoided the temptations of corruption. In any given situation, I believe that one should ask if it is the right or wrong thing to do. I trust that I did the right thing.

I have grappled over publishing my story, because I didn't want it to be perceived as a bash Kwame Kilpatrick book. Nevertheless, there are several reasons why I have decided to share my experiences and put them into print. First, the opportunity to tell my story will give the reader some insight as to how I became involved in this whistleblower scandal. It will provide the details of what happened to me after I gave my truthful statement to the Michigan State Police who were investigating allegations of criminal activity by the mayor of Detroit and members of his staff.

Secondly, I hope that sharing my experiences will give other law enforcement officers—and possibly those in the private sector—insight into what happens when someone blows the whistle. My story will give the reader illustrations of the types of harassment and intimidation that ensued in my case and could follow anyone who blows the whistle. I hope that it will inspire them to recognize that, in the end, it is worth telling the truth and maintaining honor. Finally, I trust when you read this book, it will help you to examine your life values and to reinforce your integrity within the workplace.

# PART 1

# *Character & Duty*

# Chapter 1

# Developing Character

While growing up on the northwest side of Detroit, I observed many boys and young men in my neighborhood exploiting drugs and committing crimes regularly. I recall a time during my middle school years when gang recruitment took place in my district. The gangs would assemble and commit robberies and home invasions to steal cash or goods they could trade for drugs.

My eyes were really opened one day when I observed a neighborhood boy walking with crutches. I stopped him on the street and asked what happened to his leg. "I broke into a house and while trying to escape the owner, he shot me in the butt," he explained. That really left a disturbing effect on me for many years.

I established a refuge in recreational sports and athletics. I was able to avoid the pressures of the street gangs by participating in after-school activities at the local community recreational center. I tried boxing, but my mother didn't approve of the sport so I turned to swimming. I spent my summers participating in swimming programs at Redford High School which I later attended.

In addition to continuing with athletics, I started weight training at the recreational center to keep busy and stay off the radar of the neighborhood delinquents. I soon began to notice the absence of most of the delinquents and later learned that they had been locked up in juvenile detention. As the end of the middle school years approached, I was ready for high school. I looked forward to attending Redford. Once there, I joined the junior varsity team and was playing football by my sophomore year.

The head coach, Robert Jones, was a man of great integrity, as was his assistant coach, Roy Walter. Both not only taught us the game of football but also the game of life. Coach Jones always used life analogies while he taught the game. After every practice, we were lectured on what it takes to be a man. It was pointed out daily that the decisions we make each day would affect us for the rest of our lives. The coaches preached that we must make good, sound decisions in everything we do. We learned about discipline, responsibility, respect, and honoring our word.

The coaches emphasized three important things: education, education, and education. They sold us the American dream as they talked about our going to college, graduating, and then being able to provide for a family. They promised that if we were to: (1) go to school every day and do well in class, (2) conduct ourselves as men and treat everyone with respect, (3) come to practice during the season and off season, (4) stay off of the streets (criminal activity), we would receive a college scholarship. The coaches explained how scouts from universities would visit the school and attend games to observe us. I believed the coaches, and I bought into the American dream. In time, it all came into fruition.

I took to heart everything the coaches said. I worked hard in school, respected others, stayed out of trouble, and committed myself to playing football. As a result, during my senior year, I began to receive letters of interest from universities from coast to coast and from every conference in the country. The scouts flew to Detroit and visited me in school regularly.

I didn't want to go far from home, so I narrowed my campus visits to nearby colleges: Michigan State, the University of Michigan, Northwestern University, Central Michigan, and Indiana University. It was difficult to choose, but I picked Indiana University. The head coach, Bill Mallory, and assistant coach, Andrew Kincannon, drove to Detroit and came to our home. The coach told my mother, "If he comes to IU, I guarantee he will get an education and become a productive citizen."

When they left, I turned to my mom and said, "I believe him."

"I do too," she said.

I told Coach Jones that I would sign to become a student athlete at Indiana University. Coach warned me to remember all that he had taught me, not just about the game of football but about life. He gave me a stern warning not to leave college without a four-year degree. Coaches Jones and Walter often sacrificed their time to help young men become successful in life. I know without a doubt that what I learned from them enhanced my life, values, and integrity.

In addition to my coaches, one police officer influenced my young life. He was a white officer assigned to the Detroit Police Department's 8th Precinct, across the street from Redford High School. I thought of him as Officer "Hoppy" Hopkins from the television show "Sanford and Son" (c1972-1977).

Walter Harris, standing with Coach Robert Jones at Redford High School, signs letter of intent to attend Indiana University, 1984.

Time and again, I sat in front of the school and observed the officers as they took police runs or returned from patrol. I knew then that someday I would be a police officer. As a teenager growing up, I thought it was the ultimate honor of any man or woman to don a blue uniform. I read in school how police officers risked their lives for strangers, and I found that amazing. As a young man, I believed that a law enforcement career was viewed publicly as a noble profession. I saw police officers depicted on television shows and in the news as brave, trustworthy, and honorable.

Officer Hoppy came to the high school gym, interacted with us, and often attempted to complete a bench press. For the young men in the gym, it was a bit comical to see him in uniform on the bench press. Yet, we respected him and looked up to him. He often talked about his wife and small child. He gave us examples of how important it was to stay out of trouble; it genuinely seemed important to him that we listened.

He encouraged me to stay in school and to do well in athletics. I thought it was extraordinary that he would spend time talking to me and the other young guys in the gym. It meant a lot to me to hear Officer Hoppy reinforce the teachings of Coaches Jones and Walter. I admired Officer Hoppy for his commitment to his family and to his badge.

At this point in my life, I felt that I possessed the right characteristics to become a police officer. More than anything, I wanted my mother to be proud of her son. I went to Indiana University with two goals: to earn a degree in criminal justice and to play Big Ten football.

❧    ❧

Following graduation from Redford High School, I received a full athletic scholarship to attend Indiana University and play defensive tackle. When I arrived on the campus in August 1984, I felt like I was ready to take on the world. It was initially a culture shock. Detroit and my high school were more than 80 percent African American, but IU didn't have many African Americans aside from a few on the football team. I surprised some of my white teammates by knowing popular rock songs. Growing up, I had listened to all types of radio music: CKLW, WDRQ, WJLB, even country on the "Big D."

I introduced myself to my roommate and settled into my dorm room. During our first team meeting, Head Coach Bill Mallory stated bluntly, "When classes start you're going to get your butts out of that bed and go to class every day. There will be no athletic bums on my team. You're going to conduct yourselves as men, and you're going to be winners." Coach Mallory said what he meant and meant what he said. He ran a tight ship; his presence alone commanded respect. He always held each player accountable for classes, practice, and participation; behavior in the community; and promptness to any and every meeting. Every detail was covered, and we feared facing Coach Mallory's discipline. He had a famous saying: "If I toot your horn, you better play." In others words if he speaks highly of you, you'd better perform in class, on the field, and in the community.

Some teammates, who could not adhere to Coach Mallory's rules, either left or were released from the program. In each of my first two years of college, my roommates left IU.

Adjusting to college life my freshman year was challenging. I had to study harder and work more at football. I soon began to feel homesick, like some of my teammates. I talked to my mother every day, and she always encouraged me. She often reminded me that I was there to get an education. I missed my high school sweetheart who remained in Detroit to finish her senior year. We kept in touch by phone calls and letters daily. She too encouraged me to "hang in there" and stay focused on school.

I refused to leave college; there was no future for me at home without a college degree. I didn't want to fail my family and coaches. In August 1985, my girlfriend (eventually my wife) enrolled at IU, and my college life improved significantly. She was not only a great source of moral support; she also became my last-minute typist for my term papers. She was (and still is) my number one fan and attended every home game and often sat in on practice sessions.

As a criminal justice major and college sophomore with very little finances and no vehicle, I thought it would be a good idea to start my police career early. I thought I could do it all: play football, go to classes, and work nights for the Indiana University Police Department (IUPD).

At the end of my sophomore year, I submitted an application for the IUPD. I passed the background and oral interviews and was accepted to the academy. However, the IU athletic/academic department alerted me that I could not accept the position as a police cadet. The IUPD required at least nine hours of work a week. Since I was on scholarship, I was not allowed to work during the school year. This rule, enacted by the NCAA, left me feeling very dejected. However, I knew the greater goal was to graduate and then to pursue law enforcement. I continued to study criminal justice and to follow all the guidelines set forth by the university and Coach Mallory. I did not give up on my dream of becoming a police officer. I often told my teammates that when I graduated, I was going to join the Detroit Police Department.

During my junior year, one of my teammates approached me with a serious question, "Would you take steroids if it would help you to go pro?"

My immediate response was, "No!" My advantage over the opposition was a strong work ethic; no one was going to outwork me! Along with three teammates, we started what became the "Buff Club." We started each day with a weight-training work out at 6 a.m.

to discipline ourselves to get the task done each day. I couldn't jeopardize my reputation and scholarship by consuming steroids. I had to stay true to the sport and trust my natural abilities. Thus, I never in my football career succumbed to taking anabolic steroids.

My mother often asked me, "Junior, are you taking those thyroids? You know they are killing kids."

"No, Mom, they're steroids, not thyroids," I would explain, "and NO, I am not taking them."

I knew that taking steroids was not only against the NCAA rules and regulations but also illegal. As a young man who wanted to be a police officer someday, I never wanted to try something that would hinder me from reaching that goal. But most of all, I never wanted to disappoint my mother.

I was fortunate to have an opportunity to complete an internship with the Monroe County Prosecutor's Office prior to graduation. I gained the experience of performing narcotic investigations in an undercover capacity as a member of the South Central Narcotics Strike Force Unit. I also participated in two ride-alongs with senior officers of the Bloomington Police Department. I believe this experience sealed law enforcement as my calling in life.

ڡ   ڡ

During my college football career, I sustained many injuries. In 1985, I was almost deemed unfit to participate in football ever again. With my faith, prayer, and a lot of sports rehabilitation from IU athletic trainers, my football career at IU flourished. Once I got past all the injuries, everything fell into place.

In April 1989, just before graduation, I was selected by the Indianapolis Colts as a free agent and attended the mini camp in May 1989. During the mini camp in Indianapolis, I asked my position coach if it would be okay for me to miss the last day of camp. He gave me a puzzled look and asked why I would miss the last day.

"That's the day I will graduate from Indiana University!"

The Colts' defensive line coach responded, "Sure, you should always go to your college graduation."

I recall the others players standing in the hallway saying, "Man, you're graduating" as if college graduation was uncommon.

I must thank Coach Bill Mallory who continually demanded that all players graduate and not become athletic bums! Coach Mallory's desire was for each player to become a productive citizen. I was grateful to have had a college football coach who instilled in his players the same life lessons and values that my high school coaches, Jones and Walter, had encouraged.

On May 8, 1989, I fulfilled one of my lifelong goals: a college degree.

Walter Harris (95) preparing for Indiana v. Tennessee game
Peach Bowl, 1987

# Chapter 2

# Becoming a Police Officer

In July 1989, while working full time for the prosecutor's office, I reported to the Indianapolis Colts pre-season camp in Anderson. I was fortunate that the county prosecutor's office held my investigator's position so that I could pursue a chance at professional football. As my college football career had been plagued with injuries, I was not surprise that my professional career started with an injury. Sadly, the first day of practice, I broke my right hand. It was set in a cast, and I returned to the practice field.

I was fortunate to have played four preseason games. However, I didn't make the final roster and was released. Although I was disappointed, it was easy to accept the reality of life after football, so I returned to my job in Bloomington.

శా    ఆ

In January 1990, I married my high school/college sweetheart. We settled down in Bloomington, grateful for my introductory level position in law enforcement. After healing from numerous football injuries, I wondered if I could pass a physical exam for any police department. I continued to work out in the gym and daily ran three miles around the football stadium. I frequently saw my former coaches and players and encouraged them for upcoming games.

Walter Harris (94) takes on blocker
1989 Indianapolis Colts v New Orleans Saints

My wife and I enjoyed life in a college town. Then an unexpected call came from my agent. The Miami Dolphins wanted to fly me to Florida for a private workout. I discussed the opportunity with my wife who was in graduate school. We both were excited for the second chance. In February, I flew to Miami and worked out for Coach Don Shula.

During the workout, injuries became a problem for me. An old hamstring injury resurfaced, causing me pain while running. It was difficult to work out effectively. I had been all set to run the required 40-yard dash when I badly pulled my hamstring muscle. The pain was excruciating, and I was forced to slow down at the finish of the sprint. Both coaches continued to watch closely. After the run I was asked about my injury. I stated that I had strained the muscle in training, prior to arriving in Miami. Both Shula and the defensive line coach were still impressed with the other drills, and I was offered a free agent contract.

By July, the hamstring injury was not rehabilitated, and I began to question my future in professional football. If I continued at this pace, would I ever be able to pass a physical for a police department? Would I be able to run and play ball with my future children? Should I advance to preseason and make sacrifices, only to be released due to lack of performance?

My agent encouraged me to continue, and my wife was supportive of any decision I made. The handwriting was on the wall, and I decided to retire from football. Many of my friends and family members were very shocked that I made this decision, but I was ready to move on with my life. I returned to the prosecutor's office.

Although I appreciated the Monroe County Prosecutor's Office for holding my position while I again tried to make it in football, I needed to move on and pursue my ultimate law enforcement goal.

In 1991, I applied at the Bloomington Police Department. It was a rigorous process. I had to undergo physical examinations by doctors and to participate in a physical fitness exam. I passed both easily. Interestingly, I was given a polygraph test as part of their entrance examinations. One of the questions was, "Have you ever taken anabolic steroids?" I was able to truthfully say, "No." Afterwards, I thought about the day in the college locker room and other encounters where I knew guys were taking steroids for enhancement and advantages on the field. I was more than happy not to have taken them. I passed the polygraph test with flying colors.

After successfully passing written tests, oral board interviews, and physical examinations, I became a police officer. To further enhance my knowledge of the law and justice, I attended the Indiana Law Enforcement Academy. It was a grueling experience that caused me to reflect on my old high school coaches and on my days at IU playing for Coach Mallory. Often at the academy I could hear old Coach Jones's voice echoing in a long Southern drawl, "It's hard, but it's fair!" Then there was Coach Walter who piggybacked Coach Jones, with laughter in his voice, "Only the strong survive, baby!"

My work ethic paid off. I passed the required examinations and graduated from the academy. I returned to serve and protect

Bloomington and to help keep it a "safe and civil city," true to the city's motto.

Walter Harris, running radar, day shift
Bloomington Police, 1991

Bloomington Police Chief Stephen Sharp (r.) and
Mayor Tomilea "Tomi" Allison present Walter Harris with
Lifesaving and Bravery Awards

From 1991 to 1993 I gladly served as a patrolman under the tenure of Chief Stephen Sharp. I was decorated twice, earning lifesaving and bravery awards.

☙ ❧

As the summer of 1993 approached, my wife graduated, and we decided that it was time to move back to our hometown. We both wanted to be closer to family, and my wife was concerned about her parents' health. It was a difficult decision to resign from the Bloomington Police Department, but I had faith that I would be able to join the Detroit Police Department. Fortunately, my wife obtained a job in Detroit prior to our departure.

Back in Detroit, I immediately went to the Detroit Police Department Recruiting Section at 2110 Park Street. I also applied to the Warren, Flat Rock, and Inkster Police Departments. I then discovered that the Michigan Law Enforcement Officers Training Council offered a waiver course which meant that I would not have to repeat academy training.

I attended the course at Lansing College in Lansing, where I completed and passed the criminal law, traffic law, and firearms exams and qualifications. At this point, I was certified by the State of Michigan to become a law enforcement officer. I just needed to find a department within the following year before my training waiver expired. Happily, I received a call from a lieutenant in charge of the personnel department for the Detroit Police Department (DPD). I spent the next four weeks studying the DPD general orders and procedures and was later sworn in by Chief Isaiah McKinnon.

After my probationary year, I was commissioned a patrolman for the Detroit Police Department on September 19, 1995, a job I would have for nine-and-a-half years. I was first assigned to patrol in the 10th Precinct, one of the city's most challenging and dangerous precincts. Some days I had to work a scene where someone had been killed. I saw things that would give most people nightmares. I had to learn to not take these things home.

Once I responded to a scene during a cold winter's day. I walked into an apartment building along with my partner, and we both recognized the stench as a dead body. We walked up to the third floor apartment. Once we gained entrance, the heat and the stench could have knocked us off our feet. The thermostat had been left on 90 degrees, and a dead woman was lying on the floor. Her body was swollen, and she was partially covered with a sheet. As the medical examiner tried to move her, the swollen skin burst like a grape.

I ran to the window in the hallway and stuck my head out to get some fresh air. My partner ran out the front door. I thought I would puke but I didn't. I held it together and returned to see the medical examiner chuckling at me. I thought about what a job he must have to become accustomed to this type of smell. It was awful; the stench seemed to stay with me, in my hair, and on my clothes.

Walter Harris shakes hands with Police Chief Isaiah McKinnon
Detroit Police Department swearing-in, 1994

Walter Harris, swearing-in, 1994

Walter Harris on Cobo Hall rooftop, Detroit, 1994

When we returned to the precinct, other officers noticed the odor. One female officer working the desk said, "What is that smell? You guys need to go home and clean up!" My wife noticed the smell when I got home. It felt like days before I could rid that foul smell from my memory.

I learned to stop telling my wife about work. It only worried her more. She always would see me off to work each night with a kiss and say, "I'll see you WHEN you get home." It upset her when she realized some of the nightly dangers I faced. I think she learned to turn a blind eye to the rips and tears in my uniform as a result of chasing or wrestling a perpetrator. Often when I made a routine traffic stop, the driver and passengers would jump out of the car and run to avoid capture, and I would have to pursue them on foot.

One night while patrolling on the midnight shift in the 10th Precinct, I noticed a car that looked suspicious. The driver's door lock had been punched out and was missing. Also, the rear passenger side window immediately behind the driver's seat was broken. It was odd to see four people sitting in the car, freezing in the cold winter night as the air blew into the vehicle.

The driver looked over at my partner with what we called the "oh, shit" look while the front seat passenger was like stone as he stared straight ahead. I did not want to alarm the driver that I was suspicious, so I tailed him from a distance and ran the license plate through the onboard computer. It came back as a stolen vehicle.

My partner called out over the radio for backup, anticipating that the driver and occupants might jump and run when we stopped them. We didn't want a car chase to ensue, so we continued to follow from a distance of at least two car lengths. Before I could pull the driver over, he stopped abruptly and, with two other passengers, exited the car and ran between the houses. We couldn't pursue them this time, because they had too much of a head start. We secured the vehicle and noticed that a young man was asleep in the back seat. The noise of the other scout cars arriving woke him up.

One of the backup officers asked my partner and me if the guy left behind was the driver. I said, "No, we lost the driver." The officer certainly seemed like someone who had been working in the department for years. His salt and pepper hair gave me the impression that he should have some wisdom. That is, until he made his next comment, "No, you make this guy your driver and you will have a good arrest."

I was appalled. My first thought was that was wrong! It would be a major offense to this young man for me to tell a lie and say that he was driving. He was asleep in the backseat, more than likely in the wrong place at the wrong time. I was sure he was someone's son, brother or loved one. I just couldn't go along with the officer's plan. I responded to this officer again with a firm, "No, I won't do that." My partner agreed with me; I appreciated his support in this situation.

The officer again tried to persuade me. "It's a good arrest, and you could get some good court time. It's good and easy money." Court time always meant overtime pay for a patrolman.

My partner and I just looked at each other, ignored the officer, and proceeded to arrest the young man. I had to arrest him as a passenger in a stolen vehicle. That was the truth. I turned him over to the investigators at the precinct. I never learned exactly what happened to the young man. I do know that the arrest I made would not carry as severe of a punishment as if he had been the driver or was held in "possession" of a stolen vehicle.

Walter Harris (right), awarded Officer of the Quarter, 10th Precinct, 1996, shakes hands with Assistant Police Chief Benny Napoleon.

There was never a dull moment at the 10th Precinct. Although the incident with the stolen vehicle made me question the officer's integrity, overall I worked with some really brave, committed, honest, and dedicated officers. It was a good experience, but I readily transferred to the narcotics bureau when the opportunity came along.

While at this bureau I learned of a position that was part of a security detail for Chief Isaiah "Ike" McKinnon in October 1997. It was a pleasure to work for him and with his immediate family. McKinnon was very accessible to the public and was known for stopping to talk with residents. During his tenure, he was distinguished for targeting and apprehending gang members, home invaders, and corrupt police officers. This was my introduction to providing executive protection. We had to provide security for his residence and monitor his comings and goings. Unfortunately, at the time the chief was receiving death threats.

The security detail for Chief McKinnon was a good unit. I worked with some really great officers. We worked hard, laughed often, and built a bond. Several of us were also on the department's Tug-of-War team and traveled to compete and represent the department nationally and internationally in Canada. This team was part of the Benevolent Association, raising money for fallen police officers' families. Time passed too quickly, and a year later Chief McKinnon retired.

Many of us transferred to various units. I chose to transfer to the vice unit. It was something I hadn't tried and thought it would be interesting and challenging.

Vice was most certainly challenging. It also turned out to be the most dangerous unit I had ever worked in. We had to make traffic stops where men didn't want to face the embarrassment of an arrest for soliciting a prostitute. We also had to break up or raid illegal after-hour parties. On one such occasion, we were all set to bombard a location that was suspected of illegal activities. Typically, because of my size (6'4" and 290 pounds), I was picked to break down the front door. This particular night, the sergeant told me to man the back door in case people tried to flee from the rear.

As I waited at the back door along with my fellow officers, we talked about our game plan of apprehension. Abruptly, we heard a loud clap-clap, clap-clap, clap which we immediately recognized as gunfire. Simultaneously, two bullets pierced the rear aluminum door. Someone inside the building had opened fire on the crew members assigned to enter through the front door. Sadly, two supervisors were shot but were saved by their bulletproof vests.

As soon as I had a chance, I phoned my wife to let her know that I was okay. She was so relieved to hear my voice, because she had heard about what happened in our unit on the nightly news.

The next day, I reflected on the previous night and on how sad it would have been if we had lost a member of our unit. I was relieved that I wasn't the one who was shot. That thought didn't sit well with me; it certainly made me feel a little guilty. However, at this time I was thinking of my wife and small son. We had just started our family.

Vice was interesting yet far more dangerous than any of us expected. In less than a year, four officers were shot, one of them fatally in the line of duty while working vice. The fatal shooting occurred while two officers were on a routine sting operation. The female police decoy was walking the street near the General Motors Poletown plant on the city's east side. The passenger of the car offered her money in exchange for a sex act.

The female decoy gave the signal to the backup officers, Richard Scalf and Diaz Graves. They were wearing marked police jumpsuits emblazoned with "POLICE" in bold white letters and driving a marked police car. They identified themselves and ordered the men out of the pick-up truck. While Scalf was able to secure his suspect, Grave's suspect struggled and tried to flee. As the suspect broke free and ran, he suddenly reached into his front waistband and pulled out a .38 caliber handgun. He quickly turned and shot both Graves and Scalf. This occurred in the middle of the day, at approximately 1 p.m.

Our supervisors had broken us into day and night shifts, so I was at home watching the news, when it was interrupted to say a Detroit police officer had been shot. My phone rang. It was the crew leader from the day shift. He called to summon me immediately to the hospital; Scalf had been killed and Graves was in critical condition. He had been shot in the head, chest, and stomach.

I quickly dressed and went to the hospital to stand vigil with my comrades. None of us could understand why a young man would shoot at police over a misdemeanor offense. We suspected that he wanted to avoid a two-year prison sentence for possession of a gun. Instead, he died at the scene when the police shot him. We later learned he was only 21 years old.

Officer Scalf's mother came to the hospital. I was impressed by her strength to come and encourage us to be strong. "Richard really loved you guys and enjoyed working vice. His proudest moment was when he led a prostitute to Christ." The entire unit was moved to tears.

After this major event, it seemed that the female decoys were getting more threats by the johns. The men soliciting them seemed to become more violent. We knew the men didn't want to be embarrassed, have their car impounded, and at a minimum receive a ticket. We had to be far more cautious about making routine traffic stops in sting operations. The unit stayed strong; we kept Scalf's locker untouched to honor his memory; and we continued to pray for the speedy healing of Officer Graves.

อ      ๕

I continued to work on vice until May 1999, when I was asked to join the Executive Protection Unit (EPU) for Mayor Dennis W. Archer. One of my teammates on the Tug-of-War team had told his commander that I was someone worthy of this position and would be a great match for the unit.

# Chapter 3

# Becoming a Bodyguard

I transferred from the Detroit Police Department's vice section to the EPU under Mayor Archer. Before I was accepted into the unit, however, I had to pass the "run test," which meant that I run 1.5 miles within the allotted time. Mayor Archer regularly ran three miles per day. His EPU officers were required to run with him while armed and were expected to keep pace with him. I completed the test within the mandatory time.

After completing the oral interview, I met with Mayor Archer. He was sitting at his desk as we exchanged pleasantries. I waited quietly as he reviewed my resume. In what felt like hours, the seconds and minutes passed. I glanced around his room trying not to seem too nervous. His office had an awesome view of the Detroit River and the Canadian skyline. Tasteful artwork, mixed with awards and citations noting his accomplishments, adorned the walls.

Finally Mayor Archer asked if I had any questions. I responded by asking, "How did you become so successful?" The mayor answered with poise, "Education and by my faith, even though I don't wear it on my sleeve, together with people who helped me along the way."

I was impressed with his answer and thought he was humble. I found that most people answer that question, "I made my own way and no one gave me anything."

Mayor Archer congratulated me and welcomed me to the unit, as we shook hands. My enthusiasm was obvious as I walked out of his office and greeted Sergeant Robert Miller, the unit's commanding officer, with a vigorous handshake.

Sgt. Miller was well-respected by the mayor and officers in the EPU. He ran and maintained a reputable unit. He also displayed compassion in accommodating members of the unit when personal affairs conflicted with scheduling. Miller always made protection of the mayor and his family his first priority. The EPU under Sgt. Miller functioned like a well-oiled machine, and everyone understood their role. He required that his officers receive the necessary training and certification.

I was certified in Executive Protection Level 1 and a more advanced Level 2. It was important that I complete the training prior to starting my tour of duty with the unit. Other members of the unit were very helpful in my transition. One officer, Derrick "Ricco" Dixon, took me under his wings and showed me the ropes. These guys were unselfish and willing to go the extra mile for the members of the unit. All of them were professional and expected to be courteous in public or working directly with the public in the mayor's office.

I was given the standard-issue equipment for EPU officers. My primary weapon was the same that I had since joining the department. Sgt. Miller issued me a secondary backup weapon, a .40-caliber Glock 27. The rest of the new equipment included a City of Detroit lapel pin, an earpiece, and keys to the mayor's main office (not his private office). Lastly, I was issued a SkyPager® unit, our primary mode of communication with everyone in the mayor's administration and with EPU officers. It was a texting device that allowed us to send instant messages to each other without using the telephone.

My first assignment was to secure the mayor's office and provide physical security daily. Within four months, I was reassigned to a crew that escorted Mayor Archer to his daily appointments. While assigned to Mayor Archer, I enhanced my own life by observing the mayor's daily routine. He read three newspapers: the Detroit News, the Detroit Free Press, and the New York Times. Naturally, I followed his lead. I started by subscribing to the Detroit News and Free Press.

Mayor Archer was an avid runner, and he ran during rain, snow, sleet or hail. He kept in shape. His daily three-mile run must have provided a great deal of stress release too. Although I was in shape from having played football, at the time I worked for Mayor Archer, I found it difficult to keep up with his pace.

One early morning we were running on Belle Isle, and an older woman walking called out to Mayor Archer, "Mr. Mayor, you should be a shame of yourself! Running that young boy like that!" I knew then I had to work harder on my running. I wanted to be able to protect the mayor, and I also hoped to impress him. I reverted to the training of my college football days. I ran three miles from my house down to Chandler Park Drive, down Outer Drive, to Warren Avenue, and back every morning. Within four to six weeks, I had pushed myself to where I could run with the mayor contentedly. I looked forward to the next occasion to run with him. Would he notice that I had been training on my own? The day came and went without a word, but his silent look of admiration was all I needed.

Mayor Archer paid close attention to even the smallest details. He was professional in his persona and in everything he did, including the way he dressed. He prided himself on being punctual for all his appointments at and away from his office. Just like Coach Mallory's "Don't just be on time, be early." During college, all of my teammates and I had to set our watches to his time (15 minutes early).

Now it was Mayor Archer's time. Once I observed the mayor engaged in a conversation in the hallway of his office. I was standing approximately nine feet away, and he walked over and commented on my conversation with another team member. Mayor Archer had a keen sense of hearing, which he developed sitting on the judicial bench. Mayor Archer and his family surrounded themselves with intelligent people.

Judge Trudy Archer, the mayor's wife, was the epitome of elegance, grace, and class. She dressed as if she stepped out of a fashion magazine. She always carried herself with dignity, without treating others as if they were beneath her. I noticed how she always prepared dinner for Mayor Archer when he returned home from a day's work. Their adult children were always respectable and cordial, not only with members of the unit but also with the public. Mayor Archer impressed me as a man of integrity.

We, the Executive Protection Unit and the Archers, functioned as a family. I never had to stay out all night while Mayor Archer partied. I never was required or expected to fetch food for family members and friends, leaving the mayor unprotected. He never encouraged or expected me to drink alcohol on duty, party with him, arrange dates with women for him or me. Mayor Archer was always about the business of the city.

Mayor Archer began a promising administration that had qualities of openness, accessibility, and cooperation with the suburbs. Many of his opponents, strong followers of former Mayor Coleman A. Young, felt that Mayor Archer was "selling-out" the city. During Mayor Young's tenure, there seemed to be a divide between the city and the suburbs.

Mayor Archer was reestablishing relationships and opening lines of communication with the suburbs. When he first took office, as Bill McGraw wrote in the *Detroit Free Press*: "Dennis Archer is certain to transform the Detroit mayor's office, southeast Michigan's most important political job. Archer represents a new generation and a fresh style." I would agree with Bill McGraw's early assessment of Mayor Archer.

I worked with Mayor Archer and witnessed his sophisticated approach to every detail of his administration. The office staff was expected to maintain a professional environment in all aspects of their positions. He expected the EPU to run like a tight ship. It appeared that he knew every detail of our assignments; nothing escaped his attention. If a member of the unit missed a cue, he would make it a point to remind us.

I truly enjoyed protecting and working for Mayor Archer. As a former Michigan State Court Justice, he was polished, refined, and cultured in his approach to working with the EPU, his office staff, and anyone he encountered while doing business for the city. I hoped he would run for a third term.

Preparations for the fall mayoral election were moving along, and the city was buzzing about the potential candidates, wondering if Mayor Archer would run again. He had many opponents, and some people who felt the mayor should not run again. From my inside and behind-the-scenes point of view, I felt he had done an excellent job for the city. He provided support for two new stadiums in the downtown Detroit area: Ford Field for the Detroit Lions and Comerica Park for the Detroit Tigers. The two stadiums, now adjacent to each other, compel suburbanites to come into the city. The Detroit Lions originally played at the Pontiac Silverdome, located approximately 40 miles north of the city.

Mayor Archer also attracted new businesses to the city, including a major computer company. The highlight of one of his foremost accomplishments was the day that voters approved the opening of three casinos in the downtown area.

Naturally, I was anticipating Mayor Archer's announcement on whether or not he would run again. He kept his deliberations close to his vest. I believe even his deputy mayor did not know what the mayor would decide. Finally, Mayor Archer called a press conference to announce his decision.

Sgt. Miller called on all unit members to attend the press conference at the community center at West Warren and Outer Drive. I remember that day very well; it was cold and snowy, a day that I had long anticipated. When I arrived at the community center parking lot in my private vehicle, I witnessed protesters with signs on the sidewalk in front of the building. The protest was spearheaded by a well-known community activist and local Black Panther Party leader. The protesters were shouting derogatory statements about Mayor Archer. The people who wanted Mayor Archer to resign had never been supporters of him.

Once Mayor Archer took the podium, members of all the news media in the city were present. He was surrounded by his wife and children. Mayor Archer announced that he would not seek a third term. It seemed as though everyone, even the media, that gathered for the conference released a loud gasp.

I stood there in amazement as I listened to him. "I have decided it's time for me to pass the baton to the next person. I love this city. I love our citizens, and I really enjoyed the opportunity and experience of being mayor. But I realize that I have no life."

In the weeks following Mayor Archer's announcement, it appeared that every other home in my eastside Detroit neighborhood displayed a for sale sign in the yard. In a way, I was happy for the mayor, because he had to endure verbal attacks on him and his family, and vicious rumors, and he could not please everyone in the city. I, along with other members of the unit, observed how relieved the mayor appeared to be for days and months after his announcement. He played a lot of golf and seemed to be perpetually happy.

Those of us in the EPU started to look for other units to join once the new administration took over. I had gone to several certified training sessions on executive protection and wanted to stay with the EPU, not only because I enjoyed the position, but because the schedule was conducive to my family life. At the time, I had two young boys, and my work hours allowed me to spend quality time with them.

෨    ෪

December 31, 2001 arrived, and Mayor Archer moved the last of his family's belongings from the Manoogian Mansion, the official mayor's residence. This was also the last day that the Detroit Police Department provided security for Mayor Archer. Members of the EPU, including me, assisted the mayor with the move and discussed our new commands. I was still unsure of my next command and where to report on January 1, 2002.

Just after the election, I had spoken with a friend of the family, who knew someone in Kwame Kilpatrick's camp. He was the mayor-elect. He gave several powerful speeches and debated his opponent with confidence and offered innovative ideas for the city. I had made it known that I preferred to stay on with the new EPU. This request was made about mid-December 2001; however, I had not received confirmation or word of my appointment.

On January 1, 2002 at 06:00 a.m., I completed what I thought would be my last 24-hour shift at the Manoogian Mansion. I said my goodbyes to the other EPU officers and drove home through snow-covered streets. I thought about what a good run (working with Mayor Archer) it had been.

At home, I unloaded all the gear from my vehicle, proceeded to take a hot shower, and climb into my warm bed. I slept deeply until around 8:45 a.m. I recall answering the telephone and hearing a male voice ask, "Is Officer Harris there?"

I replied very drowsily, "Speaking."

"This is Al Jackson. Are you going to attend the meeting this morning?"

I replied (still drowsy and confused), "What meeting?"

"Mayor Kilpatrick's EPU meeting at 10:00 a.m.," he said.

I immediately sat up in bed. "Sure! I'll be there at 10." I scrambled out of bed and took another shower to wake up. I put on a pair of slacks and a sweater and grabbed my cashmere full-length coat and scarf. I warmed up my car and headed toward downtown Detroit.

I wasn't sure how the meeting would go. I had heard in the news how the new mayor was young and charismatic. Born and raised in Detroit, he graduated from Detroit's Cass Technical High School. Prior to the election, he had served a few years as a Michigan state representative and was well-versed in being a politician. In the mayoral election, he defeated Gill Hill, president of the city council leading up to the election.

The mayor-elect ran his campaign on the slogan, "Our Future: Right Here, Right Now." He ran on the platform of implementing changes once he took office. He seemed to bring a lot of enthusiasm and vigor to his role as mayor. His youthful and alluring personality seemed to appeal to all generations. To the seniors of the city, he wore the grandson persona. To the youths of the city, he was street-wise and understanding of their plight. Kwame Kilpatrick had become the youngest man at that time to serve as the city's mayor.

As I arrived closer to the campaign office, I tried to envision what working on his EPU would be like. How would it be different with a young man at the helm? I had high hopes that this young African American would rejuvenate the city.

# PART 2

# *The New Mayor*

# Chapter 4

# Right Here, Right Now

I arrived 15 minutes early at Mayor Kilpatrick's campaign office located at Congress and Washington Blvd. When I entered the building, I observed about 15 officers seated at various tables; several of them had been on former Mayor Archer's EPU. I was relieved to see some familiar faces. None of us had readily mentioned that we requested to stay on board with the new administration.

As I took a seat, Officer Albert "Al" Jackson greeted me in a low, muffled voice and welcomed me to the unit. I recognized him as the mayor-elect's driver at the Christmas Day parade. I recognized another officer but didn't know his name. He had been a passenger in the mayor's car that day, and at the time I thought that he looked a little unprofessional. He looked almost like a "thug" in a rap or hip-hop music video. I was relieved to see that this time he looked a little more professional in his attire.

At that moment, Mayor Kilpatrick walked into the room escorted by Deputy Police Chief Ronald Fleming (DC Fleming) and Sgt. Shawn Wilson. Mayor Kilpatrick stood in the middle of the room dressed in jeans, a sweater, leather jacket, and a hat. His 6-foot-6 stature and ex-lineman physique seemed to dominate the room.

I had seen him in person only once before when I was escorting Mayor Archer to a debate between mayoral candidates Kwame Kilpatrick and Gill Hill. I remembered how impressed I was with

Kilpatrick; I felt that he was a gifted politician. He was a very polished orator and animated speaker. He didn't need to stop and think about questions before answering them easily and freely.

I anticipated he would give us a motivating speech as we embarked on our new EPU assignment. Kilpatrick slowly walked around the room as if he were personally examining each officer. He had a way of commanding attention with his presence. His height, build, and loud voice certainly quieted everyone in the room.

Mayor Kilpatrick welcomed everyone and stressed how he had confidence in all the officers present. The next charge I attributed to his youthful exuberance, "It is important that you all look and smell good." That said, he exited the campaign office. It wasn't the motivational speech that I expected, but it was short and to the point.

DC Fleming then welcomed everyone to the unit. I had heard of him because he served for 20 years on the security detail for Mayor Young. I also had the opportunity to meet him while I was working on Archer's EPU. Now DC Fleming was working with Kilpatrick's EPU. A fellow officer in the unit stated that DC Fleming was the ultimate authority on executive protection. He seemed to be very calm, mild mannered, and very well dressed. He spoke briefly about his past training in executive protection, how he had trained "all over the world." I was very impressed with him.

DC Fleming counseled us on how the EPU was an elite unit. It was very important that everyone was trained in martial arts and firearms. He made it very clear to everyone that the protection of the mayor and his family was paramount. Next, he introduced the EPU's leadership, including Officer Albert "Al" Jackson and Officer Kevin

Lewis. I finally had a name for the face I recognized from the Christmas Day parade: Kevin Lewis. I found them interesting in the sense that they didn't give a very good first impression. They came across as unprofessional in their dress and mannerisms, too relaxed and too casual for what I had expected to be a professional meeting on the organization of the administration and the EPU.

After the introductions were finished, the new EPU was given a tour of the mayor's office and the Manoogian Mansion. Then the unit was advised on the assignment for the mayoral inaugural ball. It was to take place at the Renaissance Center, affectionately known to Detroiters as the RenCen, located in downtown Detroit. Arrangements had been made for the mayor and his family to stay at the hotel in the RenCen for the week leading up to the inauguration. This would be the first detail for the new EPU; we would be posted on the mayor's floor.

We were advised that Officer Jackson, as commanding officer of the unit, would be in charge of the detail. Officer Lewis was the unofficial second in charge, which meant he would be the enforcer of Jackson's commands and instructions. Lewis would also have the authority to make key decisions about various activities within the unit. DC Fleming was on board to act as the unit advisor to Jackson.

Within the following days, we were issued equipment. Since I had turned in my Skypager® and keys to my prior commanding officer, Officer Jackson gave me replacements.

I was very pleased to remain on the EPU detail and looked forward to working with a new group of officers. I eagerly awaited our first detail.

# Chapter 5

# Cronyism

The EPU was under new management, appointed by the new mayor. He brought in two police officers, both standard patrolmen, and put them in leadership positions to run the unit. Jackson was an old high school football teammate of the mayor, and Lewis was one of Jackson's buddies from the precinct. Together, despite their lack of executive protection qualifications, they were given positions of authority. They had not been brought in to be a part of the team and to learn "on-the-job." Instead, DC Fleming became their advisor. Nonetheless, they were able to tell Fleming what they wanted to do. In fact, that was the first time in the history of the EPU, as I knew it, that a PO (patrolman) had the authority to tell sergeants, lieutenants, commanders, and deputy chiefs what to do, simply because the mayor had given them the authority, and no one seemed to question it. As the commanding officer of the EPU, it was up to Jackson to facilitate the security needs of the mayor for all of his events, both personal and public.

The new EPU's first detail was to secure Mayor Kilpatrick's stay at the RenCen prior to his inauguration. We worked in 24-hour shifts; I would be off for eight hours then would return for another 24-hour shift.

One entire floor was exclusively provided to the mayor, his family, and his appointees. Our responsibility was to secure that floor. The public was denied access to the floor either by elevator or stairway. During my duty there, I saw the mayor's wife, Carlita, for the first time. She had a big, beautiful smile and was quite nice and polite. She seemed like the devoted mother caring for her three boys with the baby often in her arms.

The new incoming chief of police, Jerry Oliver, and family also occupied a room on the mayor's floor. Mayor Kilpatrick had appointed Jerry Oliver the new chief, although many officers in the department viewed him as an outsider. In fact, the mayor had brought him to Detroit from Richmond, Virginia.

Jerry Oliver's family came for one short overnight stay. He arrived for the inaugural speech and left the next morning. I recall the evening he checked into his room with his wife and kids. He wasn't officially the chief of police at the time, yet I knew to regard him as such for the purpose of this detail.

Oliver is a short man, bald, and apparently in superb physical shape. He almost immediately reminded me of a military officer with his commanding voice and mannerisms. He introduced himself and asked me to bring him a newspaper first thing in the next morning. "I don't care how early it arrives; just knock on my door!"

I replied, "Yes, sir. I'll get that paper to you."

After Oliver closed the door to his room, one of my fellow officers walked over to me, curious about Oliver's request. "Why does he want the paper?"

I shrugged my shoulders. "I guess there's going to be something in there he wants to read."

The other officer stated, "No, the media has been reaming him, because he is bringing a lot of baggage, bad baggage."

"Please enlighten me on this bad baggage!"

The officer explained, "Well, the media said he has been involved in some domestic violence during his law enforcement career." (*Los Angeles Times*, May 5, 1995, by Richard Winton and Chip Jacob, Abuse Inquiry Targets Pasadena's Chief).

The next morning at approximately 4:35 a.m., a RenCen employee dropped off seven newspapers. I took one off the top of the stack and examined the front page. The officer was right. There was an article on Jerry Oliver's past, and it was derogatory. The paper also questioned why Kilpatrick would hire someone with a questionable history.

I folded the newspaper and knocked on Oliver's door. He answered fully dressed and with a smile on his face. "Good morning, Officer Harris."

"Good morning, Mr. Oliver. Here is your newspaper."

He took the paper and faded back into his room, closing the door. Within 20 minutes, the door opened again, and Oliver and family exited the room. He moved very quickly with his head down and a frown on his face. He barely looked up and did not speak as he headed for the elevators. He stayed only long enough for Mayor Kilpatrick to introduce him during his inaugural speech.

Watching the new chief scamper off the private hotel floor with his family was one of many unusual events I witnessed while working the inauguration detail. Another surprise was seeing Kilpatrick with a very large diamond stud in his left ear. I did not recall seeing him wear one during the campaign or when he debated Gill Hill.

Kilpatrick made our EPU work challenging, because he moved on and off his floor with a large entourage. Each EPU member was given instructions about his post. The mayoral staff did not make our jobs any easier, either. There were many late-night visits by the opposite sex that had been authorized to gain access to the floor.

Officer Jackson's instructions to the unit seemed to have been based on no significant critical thinking. I believed that they could have placed the mayor and his family in harm's way. The stage set-up for Mayor Kilpatrick to deliver his inaugural speech was open to the rear doors of the room. There were many gaps in the security. Jackson posted me at the side of the stage near the rear entrance of the RenCen. The rear or backside of the stage remained unprotected. I continually tried to secure that area to the best of my ability by walking to that area.

In executive protection, as I learned in multiple training sessions and past experiences, all entrances or exits must be covered by security personnel. In addition, the stage should have at least 360-degree coverage. Members of the security detail should remain disconnected from the activities of the principal they are protecting. When members of an EPU go on stage with the principal, they must avoid celebrating, partying, or fully participating in the principal's event in any way. Security's job is to stay focused on providing protection, surveying the room for potential threats, monitoring those in attendance, and maintaining a professional public appearance.

The security provided by the new commanding officer, Al Jackson, during the inauguration was the first of many fiascos that I witnessed.

Hundreds of people were in attendance, all dressed up, as for any black tie event. They were eating, drinking and partying. Mayor Kilpatrick had all his extended family members in attendance and there were a lot of them. Once he and family took the stage, his fiery speech whipped the crowd into excited frenzy. I watched as Lewis and Jackson behaved on stage like they were celebrities at a party.

Kwame Kilpatrick became the 60th mayor of Detroit. He had a large crowd of supporters as well as those who supported his mother, Congresswoman Carolyn Cheeks Kilpatrick. His speech was very charismatic. His ability to draw in an audience seemed to be effortless.

As I looked around the crowd, people seemed to hang onto his every word. Mayor Kilpatrick was a great orator. He certainly knew how to find just the right words to empower his audience. He promised that his administration would be dedicated to moving the city forward, harnessing its potential, and advancing the city's recent achievements. I recall hearing him say, "We already have a nationally traded technology company that just invested over $400 million right in downtown Detroit." My first thought was to thank Mayor Archer, but I was happy to hear that Kilpatrick recognized the work that had been done before him and promised to build on that momentum.

Mayor Kilpatrick also stated that he had two priorities. The first was to revamp and reconstruct the police department by breaking up bureaus and getting officers back on the streets. He introduced the new chief, Jerry Oliver, from Richmond, VA.

He dubbed his second priority "Mayor's Time." He described how urban youths often found themselves misguided and in trouble between 3:00 and 8:00 p.m. He wanted to increase the number of community centers where kids could go to get off the streets and stay out of trouble. He talked about coordinating this program through the mayor's office, the recreation department, and local churches.

Lastly, he promised a city-wide cleanup to remove vacant, dilapidated buildings near Detroit public schools. The new slogan was "Kids, Cops, and Clean." The new mayor had captivated his audience and rallied their support. Although I voted for his opponent, Gill Hill, after listening to the mayor's moving speech, I felt that maybe this young man could get the job done. It was exhilarating; the crowd was moved to their feet.

I was standing at my post surveying the room, watching the people give the mayor a standing ovation. The mayor and his family began to exit the stage, but he took time to shake hands with various people as he moved toward the exit in order to return to his hotel room. Jackson gave the EPU orders to stay on our post until he authorized us to leave. So while remaining posted at the stage, I observed Officers Lewis and Jackson with small glasses in their hands. I thought to myself, "Are they drinking?" As they moved closer to me, I could smell that they had been drinking.

Jackson walked over to me and stated, "You free to go now, so grab you a drink!"

I told him, "Even though the mayor is gone, it does not look good in the public's eye for the unit to be drinking. It gives the impression that we are consuming alcohol while on duty. The public doesn't know that the mayor has retired for the night and that everyone is off duty."

"Oh, yeah, you're right," he said, as he nursed his drink.

(Some of the officers working that night were assigned to the detail on overtime. Once the mayor completed his obligations and speech, they were relieved of duty. However, Jackson had assigned me a 24-hour shift. That was why I was taken aback by his statement of "grab a drink.")

I exited the RenCen ballroom quickly, leaving Lewis and Jackson to let people observe them drinking. I wondered to myself if their time cards would reflect these past hours. If so, then indeed they were drinking on duty. This was the first of many instances where I had to question their judgment. It was in stark contrast to the Archer Administration. There was no way that the EPU under Archer's watch would have behaved this way in public.

I returned to the mayor's floor to finish my shift. I recall that the rest of the evening was uneventful. However, the "go grab a drink" scenario played over and over in my mind. Because we worked 24-hour shifts, Lewis and Jackson, for all intents and purposes, were still on duty. It's not that I don't drink. I enjoy a nice cold beer on a hot summer day like any other guy; it's just that I won't do it while I'm on duty.

"Don't compromise yourself; you're all you've got."
*Janis Joplin*

I soon witnessed another situation where I questioned the character and judgment of my commanding officer. In February 2002, we were scheduled to provide security for the mayor's trip to Philadelphia. The purpose of this trip was to attend the *Tavis Smiley Presents* show "Where Do We Go from Here: Chaos or Community?"

It was my first travel assignment with him, and I wasn't sure what to expect. We were booked for a 5:25 p.m. flight out of Detroit Metropolitan Airport. The mayor and I arrived in Philadelphia, where Officer Jackson met us. He had flown into Philadelphia from Tulsa, Oklahoma earlier that day. While there, Jackson and Lewis had attended a telephone surveillance training session. They completed training on how to tap telephone lines from telephone poles and customer lines. They also learned how to de-bug telephone lines.

Officer Lewis completed the same training; however, his orders were to return to Detroit. I often wondered why the mayor would authorize them to take this training. Would it be used to enhance our EPU?

Two Philadelphia police detectives also met the mayor and me at the airport. They were white males dressed in straight-cut suits and were very cordial. They had been assigned to Mayor Kilpatrick for two days as a courtesy from the Philadelphia mayor's office. I immediately exchanged business cards and cell phone numbers with the detectives.

When we reached our chauffeur-driven Metro car, Mayor Kilpatrick made the comment, "Why they send us two white boys?" Officer Jackson laughed, but I thought to myself; when your behind is in a jam, you don't care about the color of your rescuer.

As we checked in at the front desk of our hotel, the mayor was handed his key. Officer Jackson handed me a room key and stated we were rooming together. In our room, Jackson stated he did not have a firearm. I wondered how he thought he could travel and provide protection as a sworn police officer without a firearm. I advised Jackson that I had my primary and back-up weapons with me. He asked to use my back-up weapon until we returned to Detroit. I removed it and the holster from the small of my back and handed it to him. I wanted to say, dummy, even though you went to training in Oklahoma first, you could have carried your weapon in your luggage and declared it at the airport.

When he was all settled in, the mayor suggested we go to the bar, located adjacent to the lobby. He sat near the corner of the bar, close to a table and two chairs in front of a plate-glass window. The mayor made it a point to observe every woman that passed by on the sidewalk.

"Hey, let's get a drink!" he said.

Officer Jackson responded by nodding. "Yeah, I could use one." So, as the mayor stood up (stroking his necktie and smiling at the ladies sitting nearby), I stated, "Mr. Mayor, we can't! We are on the clock (working) and not allowed to drink on duty. We can't drink with you and provide protection at the same time."

Officer Jackson then remarked, "Oh, yeah! You're right," as he nervously tucked his shirt into his pants.

Kilpatrick walked over to the bar and requested a double cognac. The bartender poured the drink into a medium-size goblet, and the mayor picked it up, smiling, and swished it around, sniffed its aroma, and said, "Yeah! That's what I'm talking about!"

We returned to the corner of the room, and the mayor engaged in a conversation with two gentlemen. When he finished his conversation, I asked if he planned to go out anywhere that night. He continued to sip on his drink and said, "We should get out tonight. Walt, what time we have to be there tomorrow?"

I advised the mayor that, according to the itinerary, Saturday morning we should arrive at the Baptist Church at 7:40 a.m. Kilpatrick said, "Naw, we're staying in tonight" and continued drinking his cognac.

I suggested to him that we let the detectives know that we were done for the night.

"Cool, cool, let them know," he said.

I advised the detectives that our first hit (appointment) the next morning was at 7:40 a.m. and that we were done for the night. I was still taken aback by the mayor offering me to drink with him while on duty. I knew from experience that this wasn't proper protocol. I saw a new side of the mayor on this trip that unfortunately would continue to worsen over the coming months.

The mayor finished his drink around 12:30 a.m., and we headed toward the elevators. After he was secure in his room, Jackson and I returned to our room. There I began prepping for the next day (staging my suit, shoes, and weapon, and making sure I had all contact numbers and itinerary). I called the front desk for a wakeup call, plus a back-up call.

I awoke the next morning prior to the wake-up call and completed my routine of sit-ups and push-ups. After showering and dressing, I called the detectives. They were already standing by in front of the hotel.

Officer Jackson asked if I could help him with his tie. I thought to myself, you're a grown man and you can't negotiate a tie!

We picked up the mayor at his room. While en route to the Baptist Church, the mayor complained about the Metro car (a sedan). From the front passenger seat, I looked over my shoulder at the mayor and Jackson. The mayor said, "Next time I'm getting a limo," as he attempted to adjust his legs and gator-clad feet.

At the church, we stationed ourselves in the green room. There, the Smiley Group provided a continental breakfast for the panel. The mayor had a chance to kick back and relax, because he was not scheduled to be on the first panel. Smiley's security officer was hard at work, guarding the rear door and denying access to many public figures.

When all of the panelists were together, the people who had attended the first session began to dominate the photo-op with their personal cameras. The photo-op was stopped abruptly and moved to the worship room, where the public was not welcome. I recall the room being very warm and stuffy; some of the panelists began to complain about being uncomfortable. Tavis Smiley decided to open the door but posted his security officer outside the door. I observed Smiley's security having a challenging time with the public.

When the photo-op was done, it was just about time for the second session. After the panel took the stage, I advised Jackson that I would sit in the first row of the audience. I posted up (positioned myself) directly in front of Mayor Kilpatrick on stage. I suggested that Jackson remain in the green room, where he had direct access to the stage.

The church was full to capacity and very stuffy, to the point where it became uncomfortable. The heat caused some people to drift asleep; even the pastor of the church fell asleep in the front row. Kilpatrick wiped the sweat from his brow on two different occasions.

The second session ended, and we made our way back to the Metro car. There, the two Philadelphia detectives presented the mayor with a bag of large, hot pretzels. I thanked both detectives and shook their hands. I advised them if they ever visited Detroit to please call me. As soon as we got into the car, Kilpatrick started consuming the pretzels. We gathered our luggage from the hotel and headed to the airport.

At the airport, we made our way to proper gate for departure. Kilpatrick and Jackson were seated, while I decided to stand. Suddenly, the mayor stood up and started running down the terminal. I looked at Jackson, thinking he could clue me in as to what was happening. He just remained seated while I followed the mayor closely. He was calling out the name of a well-known movie actress, trying to get her attention. She was walking very fast. I didn't recognize her at first, but when she turned around I realized that I had seen her on the television show "Living Single."

Within seconds, he had caught up with the actress. She was surprised by his actions, took a defensive stance, and pulled her Louis Vuitton bag close to her body.

The mayor realized he had startled her and took a couple steps back. She continued to walk backwards slowly, still unsure about the nature of the mayor's approach. He then quickly reached into his breast pocket, pulled out a business card, and said, "I'm the mayor of Detroit."

She read the business card, while keeping an eye on him.

"I'm Kwame Kilpatrick. If you are ever in Detroit, stop by my office."

The actress finally relaxed her stance and smiled. She looked up at the mayor and said, "Okay." Next, she leaned sideways with her shoulders so that she could look around him to where I was standing. As she stared at me, she asked the mayor, "Is this your security guy?"

Mayor Kilpatrick quickly answered, "Yes!" in a very dismissive tone.

She smiled at me and said, "Nice! I think he's cute!" Of course that was flattering, but I couldn't respond in anyway. I had to maintain my professional manner and not engage in their conversation.

The mayor gave me a disgusted look, as if to say I was cramping his style.

"Thanks for your card," the actress said. "I'll stop in to see you if I'm ever in Detroit again."

Kilpatrick said goodbye, as we walked back to the departure gate. It was an uncomfortable walk for me. The mayor took long strides and walked quickly. I remained quiet, as I had to trot to keep up.

We made it back to our gate, boarded our flight, and returned to Detroit later that evening. During the flight, the mayor conversed with Jackson but seemed to give me the cold shoulder. Most flights he would be talkative; this time not so much. I wondered what he was thinking.

After the Philadelphia trip, I began to feel somewhat disenchanted with the lack of professionalism in the administration. What I had once revered as a public office with high standards seemed to have been reduced to mediocrity. It gave me the impression that there was acceptance of inappropriate personnel behavior that, in former mayoral administrations, would have been considered incompetent. Officers Jackson and Lewis were in charge of the EPU, but it seemed that they did so with very little regard to policy, protocol, and integrity.

After the Detroit Red Wings won the 2002 Stanley Cup, a parade was planned for June 17. Officers Jackson and Lewis were in charge of securing the mayor's participation in the parade. It was scheduled to start at 11:30 a.m. at Woodward and I-75, the area affectionately coined Hockeytown by the Red Wings owner, Mike Ilitch, and end approximately two miles or so at Hart Plaza. At least a million people were expected to line the parade route. The Red Wings detail was complete chaos from the beginning to the end.

Officer Jackson called for everyone to meet at the mayor's office. There, we received a call that the meeting was actually scheduled for the parking structure at Woodward and Montcalm. Jackson had advised us incorrectly, and at the last minute we had caravan to the new location. Upon arriving at the parking structure, we were not given assignments for the parade. Jackson suddenly realized that we didn't have enough vehicles for everyone. The EPU was responsible for transporting various high-ranking officials through the parade procession. There must have been more officials than EPU members with vehicles. We were still unsure as to which one of us was responsible for the mayor and his family. It soon became obvious to most of us present that Jackson was somewhat confused or unsure of how to handle the situation.

Finally, DC Fleming stepped up to take charge. He effortlessly and resourcefully delegated responsibilities and vehicles. We now had a plan of action. However, no one addressed the need for a contingency plan in the event of an incident. How and where would we evacuate the mayor? We were not given an evacuation route.

The organization of details took quite awhile. By the time we had our assignments, the parade was about to begin. At what seemed to be the last second, I was assigned to transport Chief Jerry Oliver and Deputy Chief Alexander. The vehicle assigned to me was an old Crown Victoria that was dirty inside and outside. I felt bad that my passengers had to ride in an old, dirty vehicle while the entire country was watching them in the parade.

Along the parade route, Chief Oliver made comments about officers posted on the street corners: they were fat, sloppy, and appeared lazy. The overall complaint was that officers did not look good in uniform. The chief was thinking of starting an annual fitness test for police officers. I recalled reading some of the comments in the local newspaper that the new chief had an abrasive personality and wasn't received well by some of the officers that had worked with him in previous departments. I believe I was witnessing it firsthand. However, I did think that a fitness program for officers was not a bad idea.

When the parade reached Hart Plaza, we did not know where to park our vehicles. We just stopped and parked close to where our passengers had to exit. Officer Diego Santos was transporting the mayor in the Cadillac. When they arrived, the mayor exited the vehicle and was escorted to the stage, along with the Ilitch family and the Red Wings team. Officer Santos had to stay behind with the vehicle and wasn't very happy about it. He ranted on and on about how pissed off he was, about wanting to leave the unit, and so forth. I was surprised at how adolescent and unprofessional he was acting. His frustrations over the poor organization of this detail were taking its toll. Personally, I was just relieved that there was no threat or emergency incident with the mayor that would have required evacuating him out of such a huge crowd.

> "Nothing in all the world is more dangerous
> than sincere ignorance and conscientious stupidity."
> *Dr. Martin Luther King, Jr.*

I didn't spend my time on this unit looking for inadequacies; for the most part, they were just very obvious. Many of us who had worked for the prior administrations were quite aware of the differences in the style of leadership, not just of the EPU but also the mayor's office. Most of it seemed to be the lack of how to organize the mayor's security.

At this point, DC Fleming had served as the advisor to Officer Jackson. However, there seemed to be some contention between them. I had the impression that Jackson didn't like being told what to do or didn't like that members of the unit looked to Fleming for direction. Jackson would often go about organizing details on his own with disregard to any advice received. Unfortunately, Jackson's lack of experience in executive protection was becoming more and more evident to the members of the unit.

I saw this clearly in July 2002 when we traveled to Oakland University with the mayor to attend an event where the president of the United States and Poland's president would be in attendance. The venue was an indoor athletic center with an open press event. More than 4,000 people were to attend. The purpose of the mayor's presence at this event was to greet President George W. Bush along with Michigan's Governor John Engler. Based on my itinerary, the mayor and governor were to meet the president at the helicopter pad when he landed. I anticipated this work day and was very excited to see America's commander-in-chief in person.

Mayor Kilpatrick arrived at the main entrance of Oakland University at 10:00 a.m. Upon our arrival, Jackson, who was serving as the advance team member for this detail, met us. Basically, his job was to arrive on site before everyone and secure all of the details for the mayor's arrival, participation in the event, and exit from the event. He needed to let us know the specifics of the event, such as the layout of the venue, in case of an emergency. Even the restrooms had to be identified prior to the event. The advance member was in charge of letting us know where the mayor was to sit and who our contact person was once we arrived.

Officer Felix Conner was the driver for this event, and I was in the front passenger seat, often referred to as the jump seat or jump man. I exited the Cadillac and proceeded to open the door for the mayor. We approached Officer Jackson. I asked him to identify the agent in charge, so that I could make contact. He pointed into a crowd of dark suits and said, "The one wearing the sunglasses."

I looked over my shoulder and saw approximately 15 agents wearing sunglasses! I said to Officer Jackson, "Everyone over there is wearing sunglasses. Can you be more specific?"

"That's him; the short guy walking up," he said. Jackson quickly jumped into his police SUV and sped off.

I thought it was rather weird and against protocol that he left so quickly. I introduced myself to the agent. I also identified my law enforcement agency to the agent in charge of the president's Secret Service detail. I advised that Mayor Kilpatrick was present and asked where our vehicle would be located in the motorcade.

The agent in charge immediately shouted at me, "I have called your office for two weeks to advise your command on the briefing. No one responded to any of my calls. Your vehicle has not been cleared. You need to remove that vehicle immediately! The president will be landing here in five minutes!"

I remained calm and replied, "Sir, I apologize for the miscommunication. Which vehicle can we use to transport the mayor?"

He pointed to a group of vans, as he walked away angrily demonstrating his attitude and frustration with the mayor's EPU. The vans that the he pointed to were loaded with children. I told Conner to move the mayor's Cadillac immediately and place it in the nearby parking lot. I remember how embarrassed I was that day, especially when it appeared that all 15 agents looked over at me with disgust and disbelief. I just wanted to melt away in that hot July sun! This was the epitome of Jackson's complete incompetence as commander of our unit.

When I worked for Mayor Archer, the EPU always had a great working relationship with the Secret Service. Sergeant Miller always contacted the Secret Service and attended all briefings, as well as obtaining security clearances for officers. As a matter of fact, according to Mayor Archer, we were often complimented by the Secret Service.

I understood why Jackson sped off in a hurry. He knew he had recklessly ignored the calls from the Secret Service. He also had failed to attend the Secret Service briefing for the visit of President George Bush. Jackson's failure to contact the Secret Service could have resulted in a breach in national security.

I informed Mayor Kilpatrick that our vehicle could not be included in the motorcade and, as a result, he had been reduced to riding in the van with children. He was upset and asked why, so I told him exactly what the head agent had reported. Here was the mayor's opportunity to correct a major snafu. However, to the best of my knowledge, he never addressed the commanding officer about the issue. The mayor and I had to jog in our suits and dress shoes to a white van loaded with children. We simply commandeered a bench seat and made the trip, while Conner stayed in the parking lot.

It was an amazing sight to watch the four military helicopters effortlessly fly in and land one at a time. Not knowing which helicopter the president was occupying was an excellent security strategy. When the helicopter pad was secured, President Bush exited his helicopter and met with Mayor Kilpatrick and Michigan Governor John Engler. The president entered his presidential vehicle, and the motorcade proceeded to the Oakland University Athletic Center.

There, the dignitaries, including Kilpatrick, were seated down front of the stage. I wasn't sure where I was assigned to sit. Typically, this detail is worked out by the advance man, but he left. I just took the first open seat in the very rear of the arena-style seating that I could find.

Governor Engler introduced President Bush to a packed audience. The president began to speak and made reference to Mayor Kilpatrick as Congress Carolyn Cheeks Kilpatrick's baby boy.

President Bush and the president of Poland were on stage standing at separate podiums. Once during President Bush's speech, in mid-sentence, three white men stood up holding a white sheet with a message spray-painted in red: **Stop the war!** The three men began screaming "Stop the war! Stop the war! Stop the war! By the third chant, security moved to escort them out. The hecklers resisted and had to be forced up the stairway ramp. When the third man reached the top step at ground level, an older white man approximately in his seventies, wearing a war veteran hat, jumped up and punched the young man in the face.

I was seated within 10 feet of the whole incident and heard the war veteran say, "Don't you ever disrespect the president!" The crowd of mostly college students gratefully applauded the older gentleman. I recall the heckler, who had been struck, pointing at the older man and telling security, "He can't do that." The remainder of the event was unremarkable.

The ride back to Detroit was equally unremarkable. I thought the mayor would still be upset that he had had to ride with a van load of kids, but he didn't bring it up at all. I knew to keep my thoughts about the situation to myself. However, we did talk about what happened with the protester and the angry veteran.

After we returned, Jackson never spoke to me about his actions at the Oakland University event or how he missed the briefing to clear the mayor's vehicle for the motorcade. I was flabbergasted that he left me holding the bag on a bad situation, yet I felt that I handled it as professionally as possible.

I never spoke about it again to Jackson, and I never told DC Fleming what happened. I'm sure he would have been upset but at this point there was nothing he could do; the damage had been done.

Over the following months, the contention between Officers Jackson and Lewis and DC Fleming started to grow stronger. They didn't like that Fleming was working in the office. He arranged the training for martial arts classes and firearms for the EPU members. Also, it seemed that Jackson and Lewis had some resentment toward the recommendation that Fleming made on how they should operate within the unit.

I believe that a lot of the tension resulted from the fall-out after a citizen complaint was sent to the mayor's office. The letter had been sent anonymously. The complaint centered on the citizen's observation of one of the mayor's security officers leaving a popular local bar intoxicated. The complaint described how an officer entered an unmarked police car alone and sped up Grand River Avenue with his lights flashing and sirens blaring. When he returned to the bar, his lights and sirens were still on. He and a red-headed woman exited the car. The officer accompanied the woman into the bar, and they started drinking together.

Fleming was very disturbed by the negative attention placed on the mayor's office. He verbally reprimanded Jackson and Lewis, because he knew that they were the only ones in the unit who had new black unmarked police cars. Fleming suspected that it must have been one of them acting like a fool in public. As a reminder to all of us in the office that day, he pointed out that the type of behavior described in the complaint was unacceptable. On duty and off, we represented the mayor and had to be professional. The complaint was an example of behavior unbecoming an officer.

Lewis became angry that Fleming had left the complaint on his office desk for everyone to read. Within the next month, Lewis went to the mayor's chief of staff, Christine Beatty, to complain about DC Fleming. Lewis told me that it was time for Fleming to go. He told Beatty that Fleming was sabotaging the unit. With no questions asked, Fleming was released from EPU. Jackson (and Lewis) must have been able to convince Beatty and the mayor that they could take command of the unit with Jackson as the official commanding officer.

"The only real mistake is the one from which we learn nothing."
*John Powell*

Commander John Barringer replaced Fleming. With 31 years of experience in the department, Barringer had commanded the department's special response team (SRT). He called the EPU members to a briefing and announced that the EPU would be under the direction and leadership of the SRT.

The vast majority of the EPU members were very happy to hear this news, as we felt that there was a lack of strong leadership in the EPU. We were elated at the selection of another strong leader. Although we were sad to see Fleming leave, we felt somewhat reassured that things would change for the better. Barringer made it clear that he and the SRT were there to make sure our unit didn't fail. He made it known that he did not rule with an iron fist inside a velvet glove.

During this time, Officer Jackson was recuperating from a broken foot. He, along with Officer Lewis, conveniently missed the briefing. I could only speculate that they didn't show, because they disagreed with the change in command. I'm sure they must have been surprised that Fleming had been replaced. It appeared that their plan had backfired, but all was well for at least a week.

Within a week of the announcement from Commander Barringer, Officer Jackson called a mandatory meeting of all EPU members. We were contacted by SkyPager® to meet at the Manoogian Mansion. After everyone arrived, we were instructed to gather in the basement. Jackson was visibly angry and flaunted his attitude. He had a scowl on his face as he watched us all assemble for the meeting. With an angry tone he said, "I'm still in charge of this mother-fucking unit, and things will be the same as it was before I got injured!"

Officer Lewis, who stood next Jackson, also displayed a grimace on his face. We all were completely shocked that both Fleming and Barringer were now out of the EPU. I considered this to be a big mistake and that the unit was now without any strong leadership or direction. I wondered if Jackson and Lewis felt intimidated by the commander or if they just didn't want to answer to anyone.

"A word to the wise ain't necessary;
it's the stupid ones who need the advice."
*Bill Cosby*

It was early morning, February 6, 2003, when Officer Lewis was assigned to the mayor as his security officer, along with his accompanying crew. The mayor had an out-of-town appointment and had to leave early in the morning and return late the same evening. Whenever one of us was assigned to fly with the mayor, we traveled armed. However, each executive protection officer must go through Transportation Security Administration (TSA) clearance in an appropriate amount of time so that we could also speak to the pilot. The TSA, the pilot, and the air marshal must be aware of our presence onboard and that we are flying while armed.

For some unknown reason, Lewis decided to go against standard protocol and stay behind with the mayor while he attended a morning meeting. By breaking this protocol, his security clearance timeline was delayed. This was just one example of how Lewis went rogue that day. Once again the mayor was running late, so Lewis had to speed along I-94 in order to get him to the airport. They ran lights and sirens down the expressway in an attempt to get the mayor to the airport before the plane departed.

After the mayor and Lewis arrived at the airport, Officer Sean Jennings, the advance man on Lewis's crew, met them. Jennings escorted the mayor through the Northwest Airline terminal to the VIP check-in and returned to stand by with Lewis. As the advance man of a four-man crew, Jennings's duty was to secure a parking place at the airport for the mayor's vehicle. He also had to go the VIP check-in and let them know what time the mayor would be arriving. Often the advance man would have the mayor's bags ready for check-in. Bottom line: Jennings's job was simply to expedite the transition of the mayor from his vehicle through the terminal check-in. The mayor then would proceed to his gate with the EPU officer, who had received security clearance prior to his arrival.

However, in this instance, Lewis had to speak to a TSA supervisor to get his clearance to travel with the mayor on this trip. The mayor advised he was heading for the departure gate, because he could not afford to miss the flight. Lewis became belligerent with TSA, announcing his position with the mayor and saying they were delaying his travel. At least 20 minutes passed before he received his clearance and endorsement. He quickly tried to catch up with the mayor. As he was running down the terminal, he saw that the plane was pulling away from the departure gate and suddenly realized that the mayor was traveling unprotected.

At this point, Lewis called Jennings and told him not to leave the airport! When Lewis met up with him, he started swearing, trying to place the blame on Jennings. It wasn't Jennings's responsibility to make sure that Lewis made the flight. It was Lewis's breach of protocol and his lack of planning that caused him to miss his flight. For this trip, the mayor traveled without any security. In the history of the EPU, no one had ever missed a flight and compromised the mayor's security. This type of blunder by the unit's two leaders occurred frequently.

During the ride back to the Manoogian Mansion, Officer Lewis continued to verbally assault Officer Jennings. Lewis called me and tried to validate his position on the matter. He felt that Jennings's task was to hold the TSA officer at the counter and wait for the mayor and executive protection officer. I reminded Lewis that it was not the advance man's responsibility to do this. It was the EPU officer's responsibility to gain clearance and follow protocol before each flight.

After they returned to the mansion, Lewis further chastised Jennings by excusing the other two officers from house duty (guarding the mansion) and making Jennings sit at the house alone. Typically, there was one person assigned to the house (when the mayor was in for the night, there were three officers) for a 24-hour detail; on this day, it was not Jennings's responsibility. However, as punishment, he had to stay on house detail alone.

Later that evening, the mayor returned. Lewis and Jackson met him at the airport and escorted him home. As soon as the mayor was settled in, they again left Jennings alone to provide security at the mansion. Later that night, Lewis returned to the mansion to check in on Jennings and let him know that he was in the area. "I'll be back," he told Jennings.

This same evening, a birthday party for Officer Jackson was held at a local nightclub. Lewis drove a brand new city-owned Crown Victoria to Jackson's birthday party. At some point, near 11:30 p.m., the mayor came downstairs to the EPU security room and noticed that Jennings was alone. This was not standard protocol, as at least three officers were normally on duty there.

The mayor asked Jennings, "Where is everybody?"

"Officer Lewis sent them home; I'm the only one here."

The mayor then said, "Damn, y'all fuckin' up" and went back upstairs.

The next morning, I arrived at the mansion to start my tour of duty. Since I was the crew leader, I typically entered the security room and looked for the previous crew leader to be briefed on the prior day's events. However, I found only Jennings present. There was no crew leader to brief me, so I received that information from Jennings.

As more of my crew members arrived, Jennings was released from his post for the day. Around 6:30 a.m., while working out at the gym with the mayor, I received a call from Officer Harold Nelthrope, one of my crew members. He alerted me that a uniformed EPU officer told him that Officer Lewis had wrecked his city-owned, brand new Crown Victoria. (The uniformed officers assigned to the EPU were responsible for handling the security of the mayor's vehicles and were medics.) The wreck had occurred on East Grand Boulevard near Jefferson where the vehicle sustained three flat tires and severe undercarriage damage. The uniformed officer also confided in Nelthrope that Officer Lewis "was drunk as a skunk."

Nelthrope alerted me, because I was the crew leader but didn't want me to say anything to the mayor. He gave me the impression that this was to be kept between us for the time being. He was also concerned because the uniformed officer told him that he recovered Lewis's duty weapon at the scene of the accident. It was very difficult for me not to inform the mayor of what appeared to be a clandestine event.

I had no doubt that the whole incident would be completely investigated and that Lewis, being the second officer in charge of the EPU, would be disciplined, if not fired. Later that morning back at the office, I witnessed a uniformed officer using the security office telephone. The portion of the conversation that I overheard was, "Yes, sir, I had the vehicle towed and all of the debris cleaned up. It was taken where you told me to have it towed."

When he finished the call, I asked him, "Was that Lewis?"

"Yes."

For the remainder of the day, there was talk among the EPU officers that Lewis allegedly became drunk at Jackson's birthday party and subsequently totaled his city-owned car. The whole episode went unreported, even though Lewis allegedly drove intoxicated and destroyed city property. The department handled the event very delicately and off the record. After witnessing the above events and how they were handled, I knew that the two leaders of the unit had some "juice" (power).

The mayor had an appointment on the evening of February 7 with a local radio station disc jockey to participate in a "teen summit." This summit was to be televised live nationwide.

Prior to leaving for this event, I was in the security room of the mayor's office watching the monitors. As 5:30 p.m. approached, the door to the security room opened and someone walked past me behind my back. I immediately smelled a strong odor of alcohol, which took my attention away from the monitors. When I looked up, I saw Lewis walking by, and the alcohol scent was coming from him.

I looked at Officer Regina Tucker, the timekeeper, who was sitting nearby. "Did you smell that?" I mouthed, and she nodded yes. When it was time to leave, I was designated to drive the mayor's car and escort him to the summit location. Jackson served as advance man for this occasion. When I saw Lewis at the summit, I was shocked that he was still on duty. His eyes were bloodshot, and he still reeked of alcohol. How could this man serve the mayor in that condition? This was not a professional representation of the EPU that I had once served. Sergeant Miller would have never allowed Lewis to work under his command. Lewis was drunk on duty and wasn't punished or reprimanded for his actions.

I also learned that the mayor had a very close friend by the name of Bobby Ferguson, an African American businessman who owned a construction company, Ferguson's Enterprises, Inc. He maintained the privilege of arriving at the mayor's office with no appointment. I later learned that Ferguson's brother was married to Kilpatrick's sister.

I observed Bobby Ferguson at most of Kilpatrick's functions. One particular evening I chauffeured Kilpatrick to Ferguson's office in Detroit. When I pulled into the property off Lyndon Street, I noticed very large construction equipment. One of Ferguson's employees quickly closed the gate behind us and locked it, as I pulled through the fenced area. I observed more equipment and a parked motor home inside the secured area.

After the mayor exited his chauffeured city vehicle, I followed him toward the entrance. One of Ferguson's employees stopped us and said that Ferguson was out back. Just as we began to walk toward the back of the building, Ferguson appeared wearing dusty coveralls, hard hat and glasses. He and the mayor shook hands, and we all entered the building. There, I observed that most of the inside area was set up like a bar or nightclub, including a billiard table, dart board, large-screen television, and what appeared to be a fully stocked bar.

As I walked around, I observed the red carpet and sofas. I also notice that someone was cooking in what appeared to be a mini-kitchen. I finally saw the area that was used for official business, an office with a desk, computer, and so on.

The mayor began shooting hoops in a small area set aside for basketball. After he made a couple of baskets, he said "Walt, come here! This is where we have our parties with the girls." Then he quickly added "Maybe I shouldn't have told you that!"

I smiled at the mayor and walked back to the area where my partner and I had been standing. My partner asked what the mayor said. I tried to whisper my answer, but the music inside the building was playing too loudly. In the back of my mind, I asked myself why he shared that with me. I believed he was planning to invite me to participate or maintain security there in the future.

I questioned many things about the mayor's judgment and his friendship with Jackson and Lewis. By December 2002, I had seen so much conduct unbecoming a mayor. In particular was something I witnessed just before Christmas that year while he was moving out of his residence on Leslie Street in Detroit.

During the move, Officers Frank Delacorte, Brad Westin, and I were helping the mayor move the last of his personal belongings. We were removing the final items from his bedroom that the moving company had been asked to leave behind. In one of the closets, Delacorte found a black hinged case. Was it some trash or something the mayor wanted to keep? He brought it downstairs and joined Westin and me on the front porch. He wanted our opinion of what to do with it. It was heavy enough to think that jewelry or something valuable or important was in it. The more we looked at the case the more we suspected that it was a gun case, so we opened it. It was a familiar weapon: the same type of Glock secondary back-up weapon that every EPU officer carried.

We brought it to the mayor's attention. He laughed and took the case. "This was given to me, and I kept it just in case somebody got past security," he said.

We were all shocked, because Mayor Kilpatrick always touted that he hated and opposed owning handguns.

Several weeks later, early one January morning toward the end of my tour of duty, Mayor Kilpatrick approached me in the security office downstairs in the mansion. That, in itself, was out of the ordinary, because he generally called security from elsewhere in the mansion. It was approximately 4:30 a.m. He shoved the same black gun case in my face. "Walt, I don't want this gun. Do you want to buy it?"

I briefly examined the weapon and determined that it was the same as my back-up weapon. I advised the mayor that I already had that type of weapon and had no need for a duplicate.

Kilpatrick quickly stated, "I don't want that gun. See if anyone on the crews wants to buy it." He turned away and walked back upstairs.

Officer Nelthrope returned to the security office after completing a security check of the exterior of the mansion. I explained the circumstances of the handgun to him, and he stated he already had a .40 caliber Glock #27 back-up weapon.

I instructed Nelthrope to log the mayor's handgun into the blotter that was used to record all activity at the Manoogian Mansion. I also told him to lock the handgun in the closet with the other unattended security weapons. It was very important to lock up all unattended weapons, because the mayor had small children who roamed the mansion. I also wanted a documented record that the mayor had given the handgun to me but that it stored in the mansion closet until I could find a buyer.

When the next crew began arriving at 5:30 a.m., I allowed Nelthrope to leave his post and go home. Officers Lewis and Santos entered the Manoogian Mansion and met me in the security office. I briefed Officer Lewis, the crew chief, about the previous day's events. At this point, I was relieved that my shift and responsibilities were done. Lewis was now in charge of the mansion. I then removed the mayor's handgun from the locked closet and asked the two officers if they were interested in purchasing it. Both officers looked at the weapon displayed in the case. As they were examining it, Officer Victor Del Rio entered the security office. His bag was strapped on his shoulder, and he used both hands to carry his garment bags. He reeked of cigarette smoke as he peered over Officer Santos's back. "Whose gun?" he asked.

"That's the mayor's gun," I responded. "He didn't want it anymore and asked me if anyone wanted to buy it."

Del Rio then stated that he might be interested in purchasing the handgun. He laid his garment bags on the black leather sofa, removed the gun from the case, and started to physically examine the weapon. I recall Lewis intensely observing Del Rio with a strange look on his face.

After Del Rio initiated testing the action of the gun, Lewis quickly brushed past Santos and snatched the gun from Del Rio. "Why did you rack that gun?" Lewis yelled. "You don't be racking a gun in the mayor's house. I'm going to take this gun home until someone buys it."

I looked at Del Rio and Santos, and they looked back at me. We all had the same expression, as if to ask, "What the hell is wrong with Lewis?" I turned to Lewis as he placed the gun back in the case and said, "I saw no problem with Del Rio racking an empty handgun. If he wants to purchase the handgun, he should physically examine it."

Lewis discourteously replied, "He don't be racking no mother-fucking gun in the mayor's house."

This was my cue to exit the Manoogian Mansion. I told everyone to be careful and have a good day. As I drove home, I wondered if Lewis or anyone else on their crew documented in the blotter that the handgun had been removed from the security closet. I don't know. I was no longer responsible for the weapon, because I followed the proper procedure in completing the documentation.

# Chapter 6

# Vindictiveness

"Narcissists are often vindictive and they often stalk and harass."
*Dr. Sam Vaknin*

In a short amount of time, I had witnessed officers drinking on duty and was enticed to do the same. Many things ran through my mind as to how to handle this kind of situation. At first, I just thought "Put up and shut up" or "Just do your job and keep your head down." This wasn't me. It irritated me continually that the mayor's office wasn't represented well by certain members of the unit, especially the leadership. Some of the men and women in the unit worked hard every day. Unfortunately, the leaders were too immature to handle the authority that had been entrusted to them.

If I complained to any higher authority, what would happen to me? I felt that I needed to leave the unit. I held back on my decision in order to talk to someone outside our unit, because I had reservations about retaliation and vindictiveness that I had witnessed.

Within the first couple of months working for Mayor Kilpatrick, I discovered he was very vindictive. On several occasions, he would invite me to work out with him. I always kept weight training as part of my exercise routine. I continued to run three miles a day, six days a week; it was the routine I had while working with Mayor Archer.

One morning after working out with Kilpatrick, he told me about a certain white Detroit police officer. We were sitting on a bench in front of our lockers in the locker room. He began the story with, "I could never be a police officer."

Curious, I asked, "Why?"

"When I was state rep., one day I was standing in front of my house on Leslie. A police officer pulled up quickly and jumped from his cruiser. The officer ran towards me with his gun pointed at me. I immediately got scared and threw my hands up, like in the movies. The officer ordered me face down on my driveway. I was yelling at the officer that this was my house and I was State Representative Kwame Kilpatrick. The officer told me to shut up; he didn't care who I was. I continually tried to tell the officer I was State Rep. Kilpatrick, but he wasn't hearing it. I just remember that big gun pointing at me. After awhile, he let me get up off the ground and told me I fit the description of an armed robbery suspect. He tried to apologize, but I didn't want to hear it. That white officer saw that I was a big nigga, and I became a suspect. So when I became mayor I searched high and low for that officer. It was gonna be payback time."

The mayor went on to tell me how he hated the police. This conversation just blew me away. The mayor hated the ones who protected him and his family! In retrospect, I believe this was the first time I witnessed the mayor's sinister side.

I heard this story a second time at one of the mayor's speeches at Cobo Hall. It was the same story but somewhat watered down, so it wasn't as inflammatory about his resentment toward the police. However, he felt strongly enough about the story that he shared with his audience how the police mistook him for a suspect and forced him to the ground.

"He who can lick can bite."
*French proverb*

Other incidents gave me reason to believe that the mayor and Officer Jackson, acting on the mayor's behalf, could be very vindictive. On one occasion, someone tried to warn me that working for Kwame Kilpatrick could be risky. When I began my EPU assignment for Mayor Kilpatrick, I frequented Max's Bar. I would go at least once a week on my day off.

Max's Bar, which encompasses about a city block, has a dance floor, live DJ, and seating area for parties. The fully stocked bar to the left of the entrance seems to stretch from the front door to the rear exit. Behind the bar is a lottery machine nestled between two large-screen televisions. Across from the bar are the dance floor, fireplace, and dart board. The disc jockey sits on a slightly elevated stage surrounded by a brass railing. The décor of the bar features basic beer mirrors, wooden tables and leather chairs, making the atmosphere comfortable and very inviting.

Max's is a well-known cop bar. Many fundraisers for law enforcement officers were held there. This location was also frequented by judges, lawyers, and high-ranking officials within the Detroit Police Department. I met the owner of the establishment and found him to be quite pleasant. One particular evening in March 2002, a close friend of mine joined me at Max's for a beer and a game of darts. I had been introduced to darts a couple of years earlier and found the game challenging but tranquil at the same time. I always became more accurate as I consumed liquid aim (beer).

In between games that night, we were seated at the bar, when a man named Richard Winters entered and walked our way. He was tall and thin and had a dark complexion. He was well-groomed with a neatly trimmed hairstyle and thick mustache. He seemed to have a casual demeanor. My friend and Winters shook hands and then embraced each other with a brotherly hug. Shortly after they spoke, I was introduced as a Kwame's bodyguard. As Winters reached for his beer, he asked how well I knew Kilpatrick. I paused for a moment and looked at my friend, as if to ask who this guy was.

"Walt, he's cool," my friend quickly responded. "This conversation won't leave here."

I turned to Winters and said, "I met Mayor Kilpatrick for the first time three months ago."

Winters looked around, stepped closer, and said, "Get the fuck out of that unit!"

I scooted back on my bar stool and replied, "Excuse me."

He then raised his voice (over the sound of Marvin Gaye singing "What's going on?" on the jukebox) and repeated, "Get the fuck out of that unit! Kwame is a charismatic guy, and I know you probably like him as your boss, but he is a dangerous guy."

He asked if there was another unit within the police department I would like to work for.

(I thought to myself, this guy must have been drunk before he entered the bar.) I looked at him and said, "I'm straight for right now."

He downed his beer and turned to look at me. "Remember I warned you," he said and exited the bar.

I told my buddy that his friend was crazy and didn't really know the mayor. I had come to know him briefly in the short time we worked together and thought that we had a lot in common.

I remembered the time I took the mayor to Somerset Mall in Troy, Michigan, and we had lunch at P.F. Chang's. While eating and chatting, we discovered that we both had been college football players and substitute teachers in a regular position; we had walked out of the LSAT prep course; and we shared a strong love of music. He asked me to workout with him at the gym on my off days.

I became fond of Mayor Kilpatrick, and I believe he felt the same about me. We had a lot of private conversations during our many workouts. On more than one occasion, he asked if I wanted to be promoted, and I said no, because if I did, I would not have the opportunity to work in as many units within the department. I told him that I wanted to experience as many units as possible before I attempted to advance. I wanted to get a sense and understanding of the department, and one day I could be chief. Kilpatrick stated, "I like your thought process."

Kilpatrick would always say, "When I was a state rep, you and I could have hung out together." I appreciated that remark very much; it made me feel accepted. Of course all of this transpired before the Philadelphia trip.

When Winters spoke negatively toward the mayor at Max's Bar, I didn't give his words much thought. I had seen some unusual behavior from Lewis and Jackson, but at the moment the mayor had been what I expected of a mayor, although at times his youthfulness showed in his mannerisms. At times he seemed to be running the 10th largest city in the U.S. and then he'd turn around and move through the community like a celebrity or rap star. The media began to dub him the "hip-hop" mayor; he seemed to embrace the title. I had seen him appeal professionally to businessmen and then later say to someone, "Hit me up on my cell."

Later in the same year, a parade was spearheaded by a leader of the American Federation of State, County, and Municipal Employees. Mayor Kilpatrick attended the parade and was joined by the governor. During the course of the parade, the gentleman I had met at Max's Bar walked over to the mayor's vehicle, and I swiftly exited the front seat. I wanted to place myself in position so if he tried to harm the mayor, I could quickly jump into action. Given his comments at the bar, I wasn't sure why he was approaching the mayor's vehicle.

The mayor lowered his window, acknowledging him, and Mr. Winters leaned over to the mayor and said, "Mr. Mayor, we've been out here working, but no one has given us a job yet."

Obviously to me, this was something between him and the mayor; I had no idea what he was talking about.

Kilpatrick replied, as he smiled and shook his hand, "I'll take care of y'all. Don't worry."

Winters thanked the mayor as he walked away and continued in the parade.

The mayor, seated in the rear of his chauffeured Cadillac, immediately turned to his executive assistant, Jerome Fisher, and said, with a sinister look on his face, "Get rid of that mother-fucker! I don't like him."

I was very surprised by his remarks. He had smiled at Winters and offered to help him. It was not sincere at all. So, if he can say one thing to someone and then express the opposite, I wondered how long it would be before he said the same thing about me. Had his earlier positive words of acceptance of me been just a lie, as well? The comments Kilpatrick made to Fisher stayed in the backseat of the mayor's vehicle. I never mentioned that conversation to my good friend or to Mr. Winters.

∼ ∽

The days and months moved on. I continued in my position as crew leader and often traveled with the mayor, including a trip to Chicago with Jerome Fisher. I do not recall the nature of the mayor's business on that trip. While there, we spent some time at the East Bank Club in the River North neighborhood on the Chicago River. Its athletic club was one of the largest all-inclusive training facilities I've ever visited. The club contains a complete fitness gym and spa package. Programs offered include indoor cycling, Pilates workshops, basketball, aerobics tennis, yoga basics, get-fit boot camp, body pump, tai chi, cardio box interval, swimming. The facility also includes a child care center, restaurant, drycleaners, meeting rooms, and even a bar. The underground parking is a plus. You can pick up a smoothie, get a haircut, and relax with a massage.

After the mayor finished his workout, we met Fisher at the basketball courts. He asked if we had had a good workout, and I replied, "Of course, even though I had to push the mayor during weight training." The mayor laughed, and we began shooting baskets to loosen up.

Fisher announced that we would play a game of 21 on one of the basketball courts. He started the game by shooting the first basket at the top of a key. Kilpatrick surprisingly hustled and grabbed the rebound. Fisher quickly positioned himself to contest Kilpatrick's drive to the basket. With his hands held high and in strong defensive stance, Fisher was quickly overpowered by Kilpatrick's large body, forcefully shifting Fisher out of his way to the basket. Kilpatrick completed his charge to the basket and dunked the ball, displaying great athletic ability in doing so.

When Kilpatrick was in possession of the basketball for the second time, I decided it was my turn to contest him. He began dribbling the ball, and I immediately moved in very close to him. He began to throw the weight of his body against me. He started to become very aggressive, because I allowed him no room to advance to the basket. Now it appeared the mayor was angry, but his attitude alone would not force me off his path.

Fisher began laughing at the mayor and said, "Walt is too strong. He isn't giving up any ground."

Kilpatrick continued trying to move me forcefully by backing his body against me, while dribbling. Suddenly he threw a sharp elbow backwards and struck me in the mouth. My first reaction was to grab my mouth and check for blood or loose teeth. He spun past me and continued dribbling to the basket, while I was doubled over from the vicious blow. When I looked up he was dunking the basketball with one hand.

Fisher yelled to the mayor, "You bust my dog in the mouth, and I believe his mouth is bleeding."

I felt the gash on the inside of my lip and saw the blood begin to flow from my mouth. My football instincts took over, and I became very angry, because I believed the mayor intentionally had elbowed me in the mouth. I clinched my fist as I started to move toward him. In my mind, I just wanted to defend myself. He had struck me in the mouth, because he could not punk me on the court.

Fisher shouted, "Walt, remember he is the mayor. He is the mayor!"

I stopped and checked myself and remembered my purpose. During my days on the gridiron, I routinely handled guys bigger and stronger than the mayor. I jogged off the court and located a restroom to find a mirror to check just how badly my lip was damaged. I was so angry I wanted to punch a couple of stalls out but knew that that would show I was out of control. I talked myself down as I examined my injury. After I cleaned up, I returned to the court and remained on the sidelines.

During the rest of the trip, I had no conversation with the mayor. He by no means apologized for the flagrant elbow job. He once again exposed his dark side and his ability to exact revenge.

If he could seek revenge for a game on the basketball court, I have often wondered how far he would go to get revenge elsewhere.

I recall a time when he was angry at one of the local newspaper reporters. Darci McConnell had worked for *The Detroit News* for more than three years before her departure in March 2004. McConnell trailed Mayor Kilpatrick as soon as he took office in 2002. She wrote some of the most revelatory stories about the Kilpatrick Administration; the mayor frequently complained about her coverage.

One day, I was escorting him out of the Coleman A. Young Municipal Center. He entered the rear of his GMC black SUV which was parked directly in front of the center. Just as we began to pull off from the curb, he screamed, "Stop the car! Stop the car now!" Kilpatrick let his window down and leaned half of his body outside the vehicle. He began shouting, "Darci, you better stop writing all that bad stuff about me. I mean all that bad stuff. Oooooooh, I'm going to get you; you just wait and see."

I recall seeing Darci on the sidewalk, holding her umbrella in total disbelief. As we pulled off, the mayor continued to rant and rave about how he was going to get McConnell. I remember thinking this man is vindictive and has no class.

"He was like a cock who thought
the sun had risen to hear him crow."
*George Eliot*

There were other occasions where I felt the mayor lacked class or professionalism. Once was when he thought it was funny to get back at and outshine Sharon McPhail, a Detroit councilwoman. In January 2003, she accused Kilpatrick's office of tinkering with her chair. McPhail made a police report that someone had cut the electrical wires of her massage chair and connected them to the metal base. Councilwoman McPhail had no proof, but she suspected that the mayor's office or his supporters were involved in the prank. "This is clearly an attempt to undermine me and attack me, because they don't like what I am doing," she said. She believed Kilpatrick wanted to get back at her for voting against a casino deal.

After this incident occurred, some high school students spent the day observing city council in the auditorium on the 13th Floor of the Coleman A. Young Municipal Center. Jerome Fisher advised me that the mayor would speak briefly to the students.

When the mayor was ready, we took the back elevator up to the 13th Floor. When he entered the auditorium, overwhelming applause erupted. The students stood up and continued clapping. All of the council members were present, including Sharon McPhail. The mayor talked about how his office and the city council work together. He answered questions and had some photos taken with the students. As the mayor exited the auditorium, he turned to Fisher and boasted, "Did you see Sharon's face when the kids where clapping for me? She did not like that at all. Yeah, I got her ass!" as he laughed and gave Fisher high-fives.

Another classless scenario occurred when the mayor had an appointment in Lansing. We left the office in Detroit at approximately 9:30 a.m. Upon arrival in Lansing, we stopped at a sandwich shop near the state capitol building. Mayor Kilpatrick boasted about how he owned the City of Lansing.

After completing lunch, I chauffeured him a short distance to the capitol. When we entered the parking lot, one of Governor Jennifer Granholm's security officers met us. He secured a parking space for us and escorted us to the governor's office. The mayor noticeably strutted as he walked a fast pace through the building.

When the security officer opened the door to the governor's office, her executive protection officers intercepted us. The mayor thought he could just walk right into the governor's inner office. Her EPU officers quickly impeded him and told him to stand by. One of the EPU officers walked into the governor's outer office and escorted Gov. Granholm out. The mayor greeted her with a handshake as they exchanged pleasantries. Mayor Kilpatrick then entered the governor's office.

After approximately 15 minutes, we left the governor's office and proceeded to the entrance of the House of Representatives floor. The mayor then entered, as he shook many hands and hugged a few people. He remained in the House chambers for a short period.

When Kilpatrick left the floor, he turned to me and said, "Dennis (former Mayor Dennis Archer) never could have walked out onto the House floor like I did." He then proceeded to walk with a swagger down the hall, when he turned to me again and said, "I want to show you my old office, when I was a Michigan state representative."

After a very short walk, he twisted a door knob and we entered a rather large office. He remarked about how much smaller his mayor's office is in comparison. He continued to boast about how he had decorated his office in the capitol. He strutted around the capitol building as though he was a better mayor than Mr. Archer. So many times I wanted to tell Kilpatrick that he was not worthy of shining Mr. Archer's Ferragamo shoes.

I believe that Kilpatrick's arrogance was why he thought he could keep his relationship with his chief of staff, Christine Beatty, a secret.

## Chapter 7

# Mistress

It didn't take long to figure out there was more than a working or business relationship between the mayor and Christine Beatty. It also seemed to be more than a friendship. I knew that they had been friends since high school, but many situations led me to believe there was more than that between them.

During the summer of 2002, there was an "old school" concert at Chene Park, located on the riverfront of downtown Detroit. The concert featured the O'Jays, Whispers, and the Dazz Band. I love concerts and was really grateful to be working this particular day. The mayor and his wife were seated in the first row, directly across from mid-stage. My partner and I positioned ourselves in the second row, directly behind the mayor.

During the concert, a woman dressed in a bright yellow jumpsuit was seated next to the mayor. She jumped up and began dancing wildly, almost hitting the mayor in the process. I immediately instructed the Chene Park staff to move or restrain the woman. I attempted to handle this situation without drawing attention to the

Kilpatricks. The staff sprung into action and removed the woman without incident.

When the concert ended, the mayor went on stage to meet the entertainers and invite them to an after-party at a local restaurant. The mayor failed to advise his EPU that he was sponsoring such a party. I had to quickly contact our advance officer to head out to the restaurant and secure a parking space at the door.

Also, while on stage, I observed the mayor high-fiving Thomas Watkins, an active NBA basketball player, and sharing laughs. We left the stage and went to the mobile office located at the rear of the park. There, the entertainers returned, began relaxing, and engaged in conversations. The mayor suddenly spotted the actress that he had chased down in the Philadelphia airport. He personally invited her to his impromptu party.

We left Chene Park and went to the restaurant, located in downtown Detroit. Upon our arrival, Jackson secured the vehicle, and we escorted the mayor and his wife inside. The right side of the restaurant had been roped off for the mayor and his guests.

After they were seated, the entertainers arrived. Jackson directed them to the mayor's party. Other famous people were seated at the table, including two NBA basketball players, Thomas Watkins and Ray Collins.

Outside, numerous high-end vehicles began to pull up. Several women wearing revealing clothing exited the vehicles and joined the mayor's party. These women most certainly drew the attention of the men at the party and others at the restaurant. They sat in a large booth at one end of the restaurant.

I thought that this did not look good for the mayor. I observed some of the patrons pointing to the women and making comments.

The mayor left his table and began to walk toward the restroom, and I quickly followed. Before entering the restroom, I told him to let me secure the room. When I made sure it was safe, I asked him, "Who are the women at the back table?"

He quietly whispered, "They're prostitutes."

I was shocked at his response! Had he known they were coming or did he call them that because of how they were dressed?

We left the restroom and rejoined the party. There were many patrons who continued to witness this show. I then saw that Christine Beatty was in attendance, but she kept her distance from the mayor and his wife by sitting on the opposite side of the restaurant.

I observed Watkins as he walked around the mayor's table with a tray containing approximately 30 shots of tequila. He was loud and told one of the women, "You are either going to drink it or wear it."

The prostitutes began to parade around the room and walked up to the table where the rest of the EPU officers were sitting. One of women asked, "Who wants to come with me?"

Al Jackson said, "I'll go with you."

The woman's response was, "Bring your wallet."

I recall thinking to myself, a police officer on duty being solicited by a prostitute out in the open! By this time, Watkins had left and walked to the other side of the restaurant, and the mayor's guests began to eat the food that they had ordered.

While the mayor was eating, I noticed that he became agitated, constantly looking back at the other side of the restaurant. Suddenly, he stood up and told his wife, "I'll be back" and walked away from his table. Officer Conner and I immediately followed.

The mayor moved very close to Watkins, so that the two men were talking face-to-face. I was close enough to see the mayor's facial expressions but could not hear his exact words due to the background noise in the restaurant. Conner stood opposite me, and I looked over my shoulder and saw that Jackson was sitting at the bar with the alleged prostitute and was also watching the mayor.

Both Kilpatrick and Watkins are very tall, 6'6" to 6'7", enough to stand out in a crowd and easily be observed by restaurant patrons. At no point did I ever suspect that there was a problem. The mayor's body language never gave a hint that he was angry, as he smiled while talking to Watkins. Then I noticed that Collins was also watching Watkins's exchange with the mayor, who then returned to his party.

At this point, Watkins called out, "Mr. Mayor, Mr. Mayor…"

In the meantime, the party continued for another 30 minutes. Finally, the mayor decided it was time to go. As he was leaving, he appeared to be frustrated. He turned to me and asked, "Walt, did you see what Watkins was doing?"

"I saw him walking around with a tray of drinks in his hands," I replied.

Then the mayor demanded in an irritated tone, "Walk Christine to her car!"

I told him that I had to get him secured first, and he said, "No, walk Christine to her car now!"

I walked Christine Beatty to her vehicle parked a block away. She began to tell me how Watkins was groping and grabbing at her in the restaurant. In the same sentence she said, "I can't believe that he was grabbing all over my body in public. I now believe those women who said he raped them."

I then realized why the mayor had confronted Watkins. He must have witnessed him groping Beatty, who was the mayor's girl.

When I returned to the mayor's vehicle and we drove away, the mayor then asked, "Walt, did you hear what Watkins said?"

I replied, "The only thing I heard him say to one of the prostitutes was, 'you are either going to drink it or wear it.'"

The mayor then said, "You wasn't feelin' me. I was expecting you to beat him down on the spot!"

I tried to explain to him that I had not seen any of Watkins's actions towards Beatty, nor anything in his exchange with Watkins that I felt was hostile or disrespectful. My partner Conner didn't see anything, nor did the mayor's his best friend and leader of the unit, Al Jackson.

The mayor's response was, "You just weren't feelin' me, and you should have beat him down! Bobby Ferguson saw it and had a bottle in his hand ready to go at it."

The following day in the mayor's office, he continued to talk about the incident, emphasizing how I failed to "beat down Thomas

Watkins." Again I tried to explain that nothing I observed warranted any protective action on my part. I was so surprised that this was all because someone was too aggressive with his "friend." Was it only because they were friends or was he so upset because she meant more to him than that?

≈     ≈

As time moved on, it became more obvious that Kilpatrick and Beatty were more than friends. One Saturday morning during the summer of 2002, Kilpatrick had an appointment at Black Lake, Onaway, MI. We left Detroit at approximately 8:30 a.m. with Beatty and Fisher. Due to the lateness of our departure, Kilpatrick advised that "we needed to step on it." We were in his assigned black SUV; Officer Conner was the driver. We also had a trail car driven by Officer Ben Matthews, in the event the mayor's vehicle became disabled on the four-hour trip.

We jumped on Interstate-75 from downtown Detroit and headed north. Our speed topped only 95mph, because every time we attempted to hit 100mph, the regulator on the vehicle would wipe out our speed. When we reached Auburn Hills, the mayor instructed us to stop at McDonald's near Joslyn Road. We ordered carry-out at the drive-thru and then resumed our trip.

However, just about 45 minutes north of Auburn Hills, the Michigan State Police signaled the mayor's vehicle to stop. Conner pulled the vehicle to the shoulder of I-75. When the trooper approached, he presented his badge and explained we were on official business. The trooper waved us on, only after first saying hi to Kilpatrick.

We reached our destination after some hours and drove to the Walter and May Reuther UAW Family Education Center. "Damn, I'm late," remarked the mayor, as he leaped from the vehicle and jogged toward the entrance of the building. While I was running next to him, he slowed down and said, "Security, stay with the car. I need only Chris and Jerome."

I followed the mayor's request and returned to the vehicle with Conner. Within five minutes, the mayor exited the building with Beatty and Fisher. I met them at the entrance. He advised me that we were early and the person he had the meeting with was golfing. While walking back toward the vehicle, he instructed Fisher to go back inside and get two rooms. Fisher returned moments later with two room keys, and Kilpatrick suggested we relax in our respective rooms. We drove to the lodging building and walked a long distance to our rooms. I opened the mayor's room door and completed a security check before he entered.

As we were standing around talking, Beatty sat down on the bed and removed her shoes. The mayor then began to disrobe, removing his shirt and wearing only a tank tee-shirt. He abruptly dismissed us, saying, "Y'all need to get out of here. Security's room is over there." He pointed to the room across the hall. He gestured in a pushing motion and repeated, "Y'all gone. Get out of here."

I quickly asked the mayor for the time of his appointment. He said, "My meeting is at 1:15 p.m. He then slammed the door.

Fisher, Conner, Matthews, and I entered our room and jockeyed for a position to sit on the bed. Fisher decided to relax in the only chair in the room. We then began to discuss what was probably taking place in the mayor's room (sexual activity). Within a short time, Fisher fell asleep in the chair with his mouth open. We had a good time laughing at him slobbering.

At 1:00 p.m., I knocked on the mayor's door and alerted him to the time. Ten minutes later, he opened the door and said, "Let's go. I'm late." When Beatty walked out, she gave me a short grin.

Upon arrival at the center, Mayor Kilpatrick met with a gentleman unknown to the rest of us. Kilpatrick, Beatty, and the gentleman sat at a private table. Fisher sat at a separate table with us security officers. At one point, there was a break in the meeting and the gentleman went to the restroom. During this time, Kilpatrick called Fisher over to his table. The mayor scolded him, saying he was supposed to sit in on all meetings.

After the meeting, we raced back to Detroit, again hitting 95mph. When we arrived in Detroit, the mayor and Beatty had dinner together at a downtown restaurant.

"You can observe a lot just by watching."
*Yogi Berra*

Watching the mayor's interactions with Christine Beatty made it obvious to me that their friendship was very, very close, more than that of a confidante. In May 2002, they traveled to Las Vegas, and I was assigned to cover his security. This particular trip was for the

City of Detroit to display its real estate opportunities to the International Council of Shopping Centers. This convention was for shopping center owners, developers, managers, marketing specialists, investors, lenders, and retailers.

The first thing I observed on this trip was how extremely casual the mayor and Beatty dressed (linen pants, open shirts over a tank tops, and flip flops, no socks). I noticed how they dressed alike and traveled as if they were a couple. While on the plane to Las Vegas, they sat together and cuddled. I watched as he whispered in her ear, occasionally slipping in his lips and tongue.

The mayor's family and Beatty's husband Lou were already in Las Vegas. Along with them was the Kilpatrick babysitter, and Jerome Fisher, and Officer Brad Westin, the EPU officer assigned to Mrs. Kilpatrick's security crew.

Upon arrival at McCarran International, Fisher met us at baggage claim. We collected our luggage and proceeded to Budget Car Rental. Fisher had reserved a Lincoln Town Car, which I chauffeured the mayor and staff to the MGM Grand Hotel to rendezvous with their respective families.

When we entered the hotel, Carlita Kilpatrick, with the entire crew (kids, babysitter, security, and Beatty's family) in tow, met us.

"What's wrong? What's wrong?" the mayor asked.

"They would not authorize a suite for us yesterday!" Carlita explained. "We were forced to stay in a little ass room."

As Carlita embraced the mayor, I noticed that she gave Christine Beatty a hideous look.

"I'll fix this right now," the mayor said boldly.

Everyone followed him, as he marched into the VIP office. He approached a woman at her desk and demanded a suite for his family. He also wanted to know why his wife had been denied a suite the day before.

The woman politely replied, "The amount for the suite was not authorized, and therefore I could not give Mrs. Kilpatrick the room."

"I want a suite today! Right now!" the mayor demanded.

The woman asked him to give her a few minutes. She picked up the phone and placed a call.

By this time, Carlita Kilpatrick had a very annoyed look on her face. (I had never seen her look this irate before.) I observed her glare at Beatty with rage in her eyes. Beatty began to back up, almost to the other side of the room. The kids began to help themselves to the cookies and chocolate-dipped strawberries available for guests.

The mayor walked over to the woman and asked, "What's the hold up?"

The woman politely advised, "The amount for the suite has not been authorized."

"I am Kwame Kilpatrick, the mayor of the City of Detroit!" he replied in an angry tone.

"Sir, I'm sorry, but the amount for the suite has not been authorized."

The mayor looked dejected and felt disrespected, as he asked to use my cell phone. Everyone else just looked at the mayor and wondered what his next move would be. He and I stepped outside the VIP office, and he made a call in which he spoke a lot about being disrespected. When he completed his call, he said, "We're straight now!"

We entered the VIP office, and Mayor Kilpatrick told everyone "Let's go!" As we were walking out, I asked him, "Where are we going?" He explained that a limo was waiting out front to take us to the Luxor Hotel. There, the mayor was issued a key card to the presidential suite.

When I entered this very large room with huge plate glass windows, I saw an awesome view of Las Vegas. The mayor walked over to me and said, "Walt, how you like that view?"

"It's magnificent."

The walls were painted in monochromatic shades of tan. The décor was Egyptian-inspired artwork and motif.

Carlita and the kids were exploring the suite in amazement, wowed by the size of the suite. The babysitter claimed one bedroom for herself.

Kilpatrick called out, "Walt, check this out!" The television almost covered an entire wall. There was a separate lounge connected to the living room, the master bedroom, a complete kitchen, and a dining room complete with crystal chandelier over the table.

After we finished exploring the suite, the mayor said, "Walt, let's go look at Chris and Lou Beatty's room." I knocked on the door. Christine answered the door, and the mayor shouted, "Chris, how you like the room?"

"It's very nice," she said. "Look at the bedroom." (They made hard eye contact.)

When we entered the bedroom, I saw a Jacuzzi, and at the bottom of the king-size bed was a marble stand. "Watch this," Christine said, and she pressed a button next to the bed. A television rose up from the marble stand. The mayor mumbled under his breath "I know what y'all are going to be doing up in here!" He started laughing. I then escorted him back to the presidential suite.

೦ ೮

The next morning, the mayor and I worked out in the hotel gym. We hit the treadmill for 30 minutes and the weights for 45 minutes. Afterward we met his family at a restaurant in the hotel. The mayor treated me just like one of his family, including me in conversation and laughter.

After breakfast, he told me that at two o'clock, he wanted to take his kids to the wave pool. I escorted him and his family back to their suite. At 1:45 p.m. I knocked on the mayor's suite door. He grabbed his two sons, and we left the suite, headed toward the wave pool at Mandalay Bay.

On the way, he told me that he and Christine had gone to the spa, because they both needed to relax. I wondered where Carlita and Lou were at the time. I explained to the mayor that he should have called me, because if something had happened to him, my behind would have been in the ringer. He just laughed and said, "Walt, we were alright!"

When we arrived at the wave pool, the Mandalay Bay staff denied us entry, because we needed our room key to do so. The mayor tried to explain that he had the presidential suite at the Luxor Hotel (Mandalay Bay's sister hotel). Since the pool access rule was strictly enforced, we walked back and retrieved his room key. Back at the wave pool, I posted up a chair on the sandy beach. The mayor left all his personal property with me and entered the wave pool with his sons. I watched as Kilpatrick really enjoyed himself, spending time as a family man. Just observing him interact with the boys, I could tell that there was a special bond between them.

Later in the evening, we ate dinner at the hotel and attended the Lance Burton Magic Show.

The next day, after Kilpatrick and I worked out in the gym, we ate breakfast alone in the hotel and then rushed back to our rooms and dressed for the mayor's 8:00 a.m. appointment. At 7:45 a.m., I chauffeured Mayor Kilpatrick, Fisher, and Beatty to the Las Vegas Convention Center. There were cars and people everywhere. We were late for the opening session, at which Governor Engler spoke. At 8:00 a.m., Mayor Kilpatrick participated in the ribbon-cutting ceremony at the Detroit booth. He met with various business people at the exposition.

I watched as the mayor became irritated after every meeting with retailers, builders, and investors. No one visited the Detroit booth, even though it was manned by the mayor's appointees. We spent a lot of time at the Schostak Brothers company booth and office cubicle. For lunch, we ate hot dogs and chips, as their guests.

When I left the convention center, it felt like it was 115 degrees, and I was wearing a suit. My feet had blistered badly from all the walking, so I tried walking on the sides of my feet. I remember the mayor asking if I was okay, as we had walked a lot at the center, and always at a fast pace.

"Eyes are more accurate witness than ears."
*Heraclitus*

As we started back to the Luxor Hotel, the mayor told me he needed to go to a drugstore. I stopped at a Rite-Aid and while inside, the mayor said, "Walt, give me some room," throwing his elbows in an outward manner. I backed up a bit but partially kept an eye on him, as him picked up some prophylactics and baby oil. I bought some insoles for my shoes, and some needles and alcohol so that I could treat my blisters.

While driving back to the Luxor, the mayor kept whispering in Christine's ear. When I looked in the mirror I caught him kissing her neck. I understood why Fisher sat in the front passenger seat.

Upon arriving at the hotel, the mayor took his time walking through the lobby. When I escorted him to a different hotel room, he said, "I'm done for the day" and entered the room. I looked inside quickly before the mayor pushed me out and saw Beatty sitting on the bed. I realized then why she had dashed into the hotel ahead of us. I finally drew my conclusions: the kiss on the neck, the condoms and baby oil, and the different room.

I quickly walked to my room, hoping I did not run into Carlita or Lou. When I entered my room, Officer Westin was lying in bed watching television. I took off my shoes and showed him my blisters. He could not believe the number of blisters. I heated the needles and burst the blisters and applied some alcohol. It was instant relief to my feet, and I was ready for another day.

The next morning, during my workout with the mayor in the hotel gym, I noticed something was bothering him. After 30 minutes on the treadmill, he turned to me and asked, "Walt, how come no one wants to build in Detroit?"

"Well, Mr. Mayor, some people would say that it is because of the high crime and the low literacy rates. Think about it, Mr. Mayor, you shop at stores, attend theatres, and frequent restaurants in the suburbs. You even avoid spending money in Detroit yourself."

Mayor Kilpatrick nodded. "I hate to say it, but you're right! Detroit is the damn ghetto."

He refocused, and we continued on training with the weights. When we completed our workout, we ate breakfast with the Kilpatrick and Beatty families.

The City of Detroit International Council of Shopping Centers held its reception at the MGM Grand Hotel. The mayor and his appointees attended until about 8:00 p.m. The mayor told me he was done for the evening and that I should enjoy the rest of the night off. I told him that I appreciated the time; however, I would keep my cell on and avoid consuming any alcohol.

He laughed and said, "That's on you!"

I escorted him to his room and went to my room and changed out of my suit. Officer Westin met me at the room and said he was done for the night also. He asked what my plans were for the night. I told him I decided to hang out in the lounge downstairs and listen to some music.

> "Self-respect is the fruit of discipline,
> the sense of dignity grows with
> the ability to say no to oneself."
> *Abraham J. Herschel*

I went downstairs and shortly thereafter Westin, Fisher, and Lou Beatty joined me in the dimly lit lounge. We sat at a small table, while Westin and Fisher began ordering drinks and flirting with the waitress who was dressed in a revealing cocktail uniform. Fisher suggested I order a drink and unwind. I explained that if the mayor called with an emergency, I must have all my faculties.

In the lounge I observed many women sitting and drinking. I pointed this out to the other guys, and they said they had seen them too. I then noticed how a man would walk in, engage in dialogue, and then leave with one of the women. I had worked in vice and knew a prostitute when I saw one.

I told the guys that the women were prostitutes and that the johns were the men walking in and picking them up. They all looked at me and said, "I don't believe it!"

So I said, "Watch this."

An older man walked into the lounge and casually approached one woman. Within minutes, he walked over to another woman and engaged in small talk. The same man, smiling, walked out arm-in-arm with both women. The women were at least 20 years his junior, and the man was not good-looking. You do the math.

So when the waitress came by, I asked her, "Are the women in this lounge prostitutes?"

She looked around, leaned over, and whispered, "I'm not supposed to say anything, but yes, they all are prostitutes."

I looked at the guys and said, "I told you so."

Lou Beatty threw his drink back and said, "Well, I got somewhere to go" and left the hotel.

Fisher remarked, "Look at that slim goodie. (A young Black woman dressed in a beige vest, short skirt, and a multi-colored scarf around her neck. Her hair was swirled up into a bun, like a school teacher.) I'm going to call her over."

I immediately said, "Jerome, you are joking, right?"

He took a sip of his third drink and waved the woman over. She sat down next to Fisher. She could not have been more than 22 years old. Fisher bought her a drink and engaged in conversation.

I looked up at the ceiling, trying to locate the security cameras. I told him, "This is how those johns get caught in those police undercover stings."

The waitress walked by with a smirk on her face, as she shook her head. I was not in agreement with what Jerome was doing; I knew it was wrong. I told Fisher and Westin, "I'm going back to the room."

I began to walk out the lounge, when Westin said, "Hold up." I stopped at the stairs and observed Westin, Fisher, and the young woman walking toward me.

"She can do us all back at the room," Westin said.

I looked him in his eyes and said, "We represent the mayor, the City of Detroit, and the police department. Do you realize what you are doing?"

Addressing Fisher to come close enough to me so that the woman could not hear, I explained to him that as the mayor's executive assistant, he represented the mayor and the City of Detroit. "We're going home in the morning, and then you can visit your girlfriend."

"Dog, I'm taking her to the room," he insisted, laughing like a sloppy drunk.

"You guys are making a big mistake," I cautioned and walked away. When I looked back, I observed them both with an arm around the young woman.

When I arrived at my room, I began packing for the next day's departure. Within 20 minutes, Westin arrived and said, "Man, she wanted $400 a person. That's too much money, so I left."

The phone rang, and I answered it. "Hey, dog, you got any rubbers?" Fisher asked.

I replied, "No! Don't do it!"

"Ask Brad if he has any?" Westin pursued.

"No!" Brad responded.

I again told him not to do it, but he laughed before hanging up. The next day, my roommate and I wondered if Fisher really had had sex with that young prostitute.

I called Fisher's room to advise him of the departure time, but there was no answer. Westin and I met the Kilpatrick family and escorted them to the lobby, where we joined the Beatty family.

"Where is Jerome?" the mayor asked.

"Mr. Mayor, I called his room and received no response."

"We got to go! I hope he make it!" the mayor replied.

We loaded up the limo and headed to the airport. Jerome Fisher had the keys to the Lincoln Town Car and was responsible for returning it to the airport. At the airport, there was a long line to pass through security.

I made contact with the police officer stationed at the first checkpoint. I identified myself and presented my credentials and documents giving me permission to fly while armed. The officer escorted all of us past the long lines and led us straight to the tachometers. The officer mentioned that the Las Vegas Metro Police Department was hiring. He added that certified officers from other departments could do a lateral transfer from their department. I thanked him for the information, and I did apply later that year.

Fisher met us at the departure gate. His eyes were bloodshot, and he had a look of shame on his face.

The Las Vegas trip was rather uncomfortable for me to watch and serve as a member of the mayor's security unit. He and his family were there for vacation, and he also had his mistress, or so I believed. I often felt that Mrs. Kilpatrick knew that there was something going on between her husband and Christine.

I liked Mrs. Kilpatrick and really felt sorry for her. She seemed to be friendly toward the mayor's office staff and EPU. She always greeted us with a warm, million-dollar smile. That was not true any time Christine was in the room. Whenever Mrs. Kilpatrick knew that the mayor was in a meeting or in the same room with Christine's presence, her mood instantly changed. Her smile suddenly became a scowl. Her cheerful disposition became clouded with anger and jealousy. She was disturbed by the constant meetings between the mayor and Christine. Whenever she called the office after hours and I answered the phone, the conversation was brief. She would ask in a demanding tone, "Walt, where's Kwame?" I would respond "In a meeting." She would snap back "Who is in there with him?" My response was simple, "No one but Christine." If I asked if she wanted me to interrupt them, she would snap back, "No" and immediately hang up.

Mrs. Kilpatrick's demeanor towards anyone around her when Christine was in the room or nearby was palpable. I felt that if she knew some of the things I saw and heard, she would have ended their marriage.

I recall one Saturday evening when she wanted to have dinner with her husband. It was early in the evening with plenty of time to go to dinner and maybe see a movie. The EPU was on downtime, which meant that we were not expecting to leave the house and were in a relaxed mode. I was in the security office of the mansion, and the mayor was in the nearby entertainment room watching television. The entertainment room had theatre-style seating, a large-screen television, and full surround-sound system.

Mrs. Kilpatrick was upstairs. She called the security office. "Where's Kwame?" she asked.

I told her, and she requested that I ask if he wanted to go out to dinner with her.

"No." The mayor's eyes were locked on the television. He didn't pause to think about the request, and he didn't look at me.

I told Mrs. Kilpatrick his response. She immediately hung up the phone, and moments later I heard her coming downstairs. She marched into the entertainment room and had a verbal exchange with the mayor. I couldn't hear exactly what they said, only that the voices were raised enough to know that there was some sort of debate going on over dinner.

Mrs. Kilpatrick then stormed out of the room and stomped up the stairs, showing that she was either hurt, very upset, or both. Shortly after, the phone rang again. I picked it up. It was the mayor. "Be ready to go in 20 minutes." I smiled and thought that Mrs. Kilpatrick must have won the argument.

I was at the garage on standby, fully expecting the mayor and his wife to come out. To my surprise, he was alone. He told me to take him to his office.

When we arrived there, Kilpatrick went to his private office, and I waited in the vestibule. Without delay, Christine arrived from the rear elevators, carrying a plate of food in each hand. The plates were similar to those we would often find along with silverware and champagne glasses in the back of the mayor's city-owned vehicles. The plates were not Styrofoam or paper but appeared to be fine china or "regular" dinner plates.

Christine was also carrying a bottle of wine or champagne. It didn't take much for me to understand what the mayor preferred to do that evening. He had declined his wife's invitation for dinner in lieu of dinner with Christine.

Did Lou Beatty have any suspicions of what was going on between his wife and the mayor? Lou was a soft-spoken man who had known the mayor for years. They seemed to be good friends. They often worked out at the same gym and both had a big muscular build. Although he seemed mild-mannered, there were many times when I was concerned that I might have to use physical force on him in the line of duty. Many of us on the EPU feared the day that Mr. Beatty would find his wife in an inappropriate situation with the mayor. It was common knowledge that he and his wife often argued but would make up later after Lou sent her flowers.

Christine spent countless hours with the mayor outside of normal business hours, and this would often anger Lou. Unlike the mayor's wife who would call the office after business hours, Lou knew about the frequent office meetings, but I think he didn't know about the meetings at his home.

Meetings between Christine and the mayor were held many times in the late evening hours at her home. The meetings were held on the pretense of business that couldn't be done in the office. His visits were brief, lasting at most an hour, yet they were always timed while Lou worked the afternoon shift at a local plant. At no time were EPU personnel allowed in Christine's home. In order to secure the mayor, we waited outside.

Most of the time, we tried to develop a plan on how to handle Lou Beatty should he unexpectedly return home. Would he be angry? Should we stop him from entering his own home? Should we go inside and warn the mayor that Lou was coming? We would discuss these scenarios and our available options. We decided that if Lou Beatty were to return unexpectedly, one of us would detain him in the driveway and the other would go inside to inform the mayor. Fortunately, out of all the visits to Beattys' home, we never needed such a back-up plan. Yet, it was just another example of the compromising positions that the mayor often would put us in while he carried out his transgressions.

ॐ    ॐ

The EPU faced many of these situations during the times the mayor was in Detroit, as well as when he traveled. In September 2002, he was expected to attend an event in Washington, D.C. One day in his office, he said he would like to hang out at specific nightclub while in DC. He then told Jerome Fisher, who was standing in the hallway near security office, "Walt's going to like that nightclub. Wait until he see all the bad hammers (beautiful women)." The mayor was really happy with the thought of going to that nightclub.

I entered the security office and called the EPU in Washington, D.C. I spoke with Commanding Officer Peter Thompson and thanked him for assigning an officer to Mayor Kilpatrick. I also asked the status of the nightclub, because the mayor planned to visit it. The commander immediately said, "That club is currently under investigation and off-limits to all of our officers."

I thanked him for that information and said that I would pass it along to Mayor Kilpatrick. I went to the mayor's inner office and relayed the information from the commander. The mayor became dejected but said he understood.

The purpose of the DC trip was to attend the Congressional Black Caucus. For this particular trip, I traveled with Kilpatrick, Beatty, and Lewis. Also attending the caucus were Kilpatrick's appointees, including Amy Malone, Carlita's college friend.

During the caucus, the mayor's father, Bernard Kilpatrick, joined us. Upon arrival at Reagan National Airport, a limo was waiting for us. Louis, the chauffeur, was an average-sized man with dark skin and a heavy Virgin Islands accent. According to my receipt, the limo was reserved by Mayor Kilpatrick and was billed to the City of Detroit from the time we arrived to Washington until we departed. We were transported to the hotel and given our room assignments. The mayor was on the 12th floor, Beatty on the 9th floor, and Lewis and I shared a room on the 6th floor.

The Washington Police Department's EPU assigned Sgt. Mahoney to assist us during our visit. The mayor's appointees met us in the hotel lobby. He turned to Lewis and said, "Carlita sent Amy Malone to watch me!"

Lewis replied, "Yeah, I know."

Kilpatrick then said, "When we take the limo, we'll get rid of her!" He entered one of the ballrooms for a meeting with the appointees and to delegate certain duties to them.

Lewis and I escorted the mayor to his room and then went to our room. Lewis said he couldn't wait to go to the nightclub. I warned him that the nightclub was off-limits, according to Commander Thompson. Lewis said that the mayor had been talking about going to the club that morning. "If the mayor wants to go to the club, it's our job as bodyguards to take him to the club!"

I was perplexed at Lewis's statement.

                    ❧   ☙

We spent the first day, September 12, 2002, attending various receptions.

The next morning, I received the wake-up call I had ordered the night before. Lewis did not want to get out of bed. I checked the itinerary for the day and called Louis, the limo driver. I told him the mayor's first hit (appointment) was at 10:00 a.m. I then completed my exercise routine, because Kilpatrick had no plans to work out. During my entire workout, Lewis stayed in bed and complained that working out was overrated.

After I showered and quickly dressed, I encouraged him to hurry, because I wanted to arrive at the mayor's room early. I always remained professional and prompt and never wanted to make the mayor wait.

While I continued to wait for Lewis to get ready, he asked, "Who in the unit needs to go?"

"What do you mean?"

"I think Nelthrope needs to go! We need to get rid of him!"

"He's been doing a very good job," I responded, "and the mayor and the First Lady (Carlita Kilpatrick) love him."

"Naw, he has to go!" Lewis insisted.

I ended the conversation by saying, "Speaking of go, let's get out of here and get up to the mayor's room."

It was 8:45 a.m. when we arrived at his room. We stood outside his door for approximately 15 minutes. I recall hearing the mayor and Christine engaged in a conversation inside the room.

Lewis began laughing. "Walt, man, she stayed the night! She stayed the night!" He spoke while covering his mouth with his hand.

Kilpatrick suddenly burst out of his room and slammed the door, hollering, "Let's go!"

We took the elevator to the lobby and found a breakfast buffet. I called Louis. He said that he was waiting for us in front of the hotel. When the mayor finished eating, he asked if I had the itinerary. I reached inside my suit jacket and gave it to him.

At 9:45 a.m., we entered the limo and advised Louis to head to the Washington Convention Center. He assured me that we would make it on time, because he knew all the shortcuts.

Upon arrival at the center, Kilpatrick met his mother who was holding an issue forum on "Raising Successful Black Men." The guest speakers were Mayor Kilpatrick and Jason Mitchell.

Room 25 was packed, standing room only. The mayor and Mitchell shook hands in the hallway and spoke briefly. Mitchell wore a black suit with a white shirt and designer sunglasses, which he continued to sport inside the forum. Before entering the room,

Mitchell turned to the mayor and said, "I really want to do something with you in the community."

When they entered the room, everyone started applauding. The congresswoman had to quiet the audience, because they became noisy during the photo op. There were so many people in the room that the doors had to be opened to allow the air to circulate.

As the forum ended, the audience rushed Mayor Kilpatrick and Jason Mitchell. Lewis and I had a challenging time holding back the audience plus the crowd that came from the overflow rooms. Most of the people were excited to see and take pictures with Mitchell but not so much with the mayor.

We returned to our hotel shortly after noon. At 5:00 p.m., Lewis and I began to dress for the black tie event. We wore black suits, white shirts, and black ties. We saved our bowties for Saturday's black tie event. We left to pick up Mayor Kilpatrick.

We arrived at his room and awaited his departure. Soon he exited his room, asking, "How I look?"

"Sugar sharp," I told him. He wore a very expensive black suit, diamond stud in his left ear, and his Detroit-famous black gator shoes. While walking to the elevator, the mayor said, "Tomorrow I need to go to a men's formal store for some new cufflinks."

When we arrived downstairs at the reception hosted by the National Organization of Concerned Black Men, the mayor walked in, shook a couple of hands, and then we headed for the limo.

We attended the VIP pre-gala reception for 100 Black Men of America. The mayor shook hands, posed for some pictures, and held a couple of brief conversations. We then went to the limo and headed for the Hard Rock Café for the DTE Michigan Celebration, co-hosted by Congresswoman Carolyn Cheeks Kilpatrick, Congressman John Conyers, and Mayor Kilpatrick.

When we arrived at the Hard Rock Café at 7:25 p.m., it was packed, shoulder to shoulder. I recall saying to Lewis as we left the limo, "Look at the crowd, Lewis! We'll use tight coverage on the mayor."

We entered the restaurant and moved Kilpatrick through the crowd. We used a passive push to get him through, but people continued to reach out to shake his hand. The crowd began to shout "Detroit! Detroit!"

The mayor raised the roof (pumping his hand in the air) as the crowd shouted "Detroit!" We moved the mayor toward the stage to join Congresswoman Kilpatrick. The crowd began to cheer louder as Mayor Kilpatrick whipped them into frenzy with his presence.

I looked at the other end of the stage and observed a famous Black actor dressed all in black. He walked across the stage, and the crowd went wild again as he waved and blew kisses. Mayor Kilpatrick met him center stage, and they exchanged handshakes and brotherly hugs. I observed the appointees and many prominent Detroiters in the crowd.

The congresswoman and the mayor made short speeches, and then Mayor Kilpatrick walked around, shook hands, took pictures, and had a few drinks. Amy Malone made it a point to follow the mayor, as he walked around the Hard Rock Café.

At 10:30 p.m., Mayor Kilpatrick turned to Fisher and said, "We're going to lose Carlita's watchdog." He walked over to Christine and whispered in her ear. He then said goodbye to his mother, and we headed for the limo. I told Sgt. Mahoney that we were going back to the hotel to get out of our formal attire.

I changed into a cream-colored, short-sleeve summer sweater and tan slacks. Lewis put on a white, long-sleeve shirt and tan pants. "Where does the mayor want to go?" I asked him.

He replied, "He just wants to get out!"

Lewis and I arrived at the mayor's room at 11:20 p.m. He exited wearing a short-sleeve, cream-colored knit shirt, navy blue slacks, and navy blue gators. As we waited for the elevator, he commented that the actor back at the Hard Rock Café had some serious body odor. "That cat must have worked out, got funky and came straight over to Hard Rock."

When we arrived in the lobby, Fisher was waiting for us.

"Hey, Jerome, did you smell old-boy?" the mayor asked.

"He was kicking!" Fisher replied.

"Let's head to the nightclub," the mayor said as we exited the hotel.

I was completely shocked and dumbfounded at the mayor's decision. Lewis and Fisher both became excited and agreed. "Yeah, that's my dog!"

Before I entered the limo, I advised Sgt. Mahoney of the mayor's decision to visit the nightclub. "I cannot and will not go in there!" Sgt. Mahoney responded. "That nightclub is off-limits to DC police officers."

I told Sgt. Mahoney that I had informed the mayor of Commander Thompson's warning about the club. I then witnessed a number of females entering Sgt. Mahoney's unmarked unit. Those were the same women from the Detroit party at the Hard Rock Café.

Shortly after midnight, the limo arrived at the nightclub with Sgt. Mahoney in tow. As we pulled up to the entrance, Louis looked over at me and cautioned in his fine Caribbean accent, "There's a lot of people there. Be careful on the inside."

A long line, mostly scantily dressed women, was wrapped around the big building. When the limo stopped, people began to approach, wondering who was inside. I quickly exited the limo and walked to the rear door. I politely asked people to step away, as I gave a pushing motion with my hands. I was relieved that the people complied with my verbal command. I recall thinking the mayor had made a terrible decision. I noticed that the nightclub had approximately six security personnel with wands (hand-held metal detectors). My main concern then was speaking to the manager or owner about entering the club armed.

The mayor was ready to exit the limo, and I told Lewis to stand by with him. I approached the security officer and asked if the manager was present. He asked me to wait a minute and shortly returned with a man who said, "I'm the manager. How can I help you?"

There were so many people present, staring down my throat, that I repositioned my body allowing me to speak to the manager so that my voice was somewhat camouflaged. I identified myself and alerted him that Lewis and I were armed police officers providing protection for Mayor Kilpatrick of Detroit. I explained that Kilpatrick wanted to visit the club, and we would escort him inside.

The manager said that we could not enter the club with weapons, law enforcement or not. I politely said that I understood and requested to speak to the owner.

The manager said he would see if the owner was available. He ran up the ramp and into the club. By this time Kilpatrick was stepping out of the limo. I signaled Lewis to hold the mayor at the limo.

The manager returned with a light-complexioned man who had four women with him, two on each side. He stated as he approached me directly, "That's him right there."

I watched as the owner approached walking with a wide-legged strut and a pompous look. "I'm the owner," he said, now flanked by four women and two security officers. "How can I help you?"

Once again the large crowd came too close, staring at me, waiting for my response. I asked the owner if we could step away from the crowd and talk.

"No, we can talk right here!" he said, pointing to the ground.

I took a look around, repositioned my body, and with a shallow voice identified myself. I advised that Lewis and I were both armed and would escort Mayor Kilpatrick inside.

"Ain't no guns coming inside the club, even if you are police officers," he said.

I politely thanked him and walked back to the limo. Before I could reach the limo, the mayor, Fisher, and Lewis met me in the road. I immediately informed the mayor, "We're not going inside. Let's get back in the limo."

"What's the problem?" the mayor asked.

I explained that the owner would not allow armed police officers inside the club. Kilpatrick began to observe the women in line and said wait a minute. He walked toward the owner. The owner then made a suggestion to Lewis and me: "Y'all can give us your guns, and we will put them in a lockbox. You will have a key, and we will have a key, so if you need your gun we can get it for you."

I immediately replied, "No, that's not going to work. Mr. Mayor, let's get back in the limo." I put my hand in the small of his back.

Officer Lewis blurted out, "Walt, let's just give them our guns."

"Lewis, you can't surrender your weapon to a civilian," I quickly responded, "certainly not to a nightclub owner."

Sgt. Mahoney stood by his vehicle and watched this whole charade.

I repeated, "Mr. Mayor, let's get in the limo and get out of here."

We started walking back to the limo when Lewis blurted out, "Walt, I can give you my gun, and Jerome and I can take the mayor into the club. You can wait in the limo with the guns."

Kilpatrick looked back at the women in line and said, "Yeah, Lewis, let's do that!"

I looked the mayor in the eyes and said, "Mr. Mayor, I strongly advise against this decision."

Lewis removed his weapon and handed it to me. I accepted it and saw how hell-bent the mayor was on going into the club at any cost. I stood by watching the mayor, Fisher, Lewis, and the carload of women walk to the front of the line and enter the club.

I walked over to Sgt. Mahoney and before I could say anything, he said, "Man, I'm glad you didn't give them your gun. I'm out of here, man. We're not allowed to go into that club."

I sat in the limo with Lewis's gun and waited for him and the others to return. I prayed that no harm would come to the mayor, as I sat listening to the boisterous crowd outside. I could not comprehend how someone with a college degree, law degree, and title of mayor could make such an immature decision.

At almost 2:00 a.m., the mayor returned to the limo with Fisher and Lewis. As they were talking in loud voices about the women inside, I could tell that they were inebriated. Lewis stood close to me. "Man, something broke out in there. You know, we needed you. There was this drunken guy inside trying to get at the mayor, but Jerome and I handled him until security arrived."

"That's why I opposed taking the mayor inside the club," I said. I thought, this Lewis idiot is drunk and dangerous. He asked for his gun, as the mayor and Fisher entered the limo. I kept my head on swivel, as I noticed the people outside the club began to act disorderly. I entered the front passenger seat of the limo and told Louis to hurry and pull off.

I picked up the limo phone and pressed the line for the phone in the rear of the vehicle. Lewis answered and I said, "Where does the mayor want to go?"

"Hold on, man," he said. All I could hear was the mayor and Fisher talking about some female buttocks. Lewis returned to the line and said, "Tell the driver the mayor wants to go to Ben's Chili Bowl."

A few minutes later, we arrived at the restaurant. I observed many people who appeared to be intoxicated. I walked very close to Mayor Kilpatrick as we looked for an empty table. A waitress was wiping down an empty table, and she motioned that it was available for seating. I commandeered the table as Fisher and Lewis sat down. The mayor continued standing as he was busy texting on his Skypager®, with a mischievous grin on his face.

He walked over to the counter and ordered some chili and turkey sausages. I thought that was a lot of food for one person. Kilpatrick returned to the table and sat down next to Fisher. I really felt uncomfortable in this crowded restaurant. I noticed some unsavory characters seated near our table. My mental state was condition red. I was fully alert, expecting an incident to happen and was ready to act.

Lewis was in another world, as he asked if I wanted a sausage. I gritted my teeth and told him, "You enjoy your sausage. My attention is on the mayor."

I observed more intoxicated people entering the restaurant, and they appeared to be the gangster/hood variety. I was not afraid of the people in the restaurant, but the ambiance was primed for a potential problem. The mayor talked, texted, and ate before we left at 4:00 a.m.

When we were on our way to the limo, Kilpatrick was carrying a bag of food. I thought, gosh, is he going to eat again?

Back at the hotel, Lewis and I escorted Kilpatrick to his room. I thought it was odd that before he opened his door, he turned at us and said, "Y'all gone now. I got this."

I looked at Lewis, and he looked at me puzzled. Mayor Kilpatrick opened the door, stepped inside, closing the room door quickly. I looked at Lewis and asked, "What was that all about?" He shrugged his shoulders and we walked off to the elevator.

The next morning the mayor, Lewis, and I went to the hotel's fitness center. We worked out and then went to the breakfast buffet. The mayor reminded us that he needed to buy some cufflinks. He said later he would call us when he was ready to go.

We took the elevator back to the 12th Floor, and when we began to exit the elevator, Kilpatrick started running in an all-out sprint. Visualize a man 6'6", 320 pounds, barreling down the hallway in sweats and gym shoes. Lewis and I immediately followed him in an all-out sprint. "What's going on?" I asked.

"I don't know."

"Mr. Mayor! Mr. Mayor!" I shouted. "What's the problem?"

He continued running as he peeked back at us to check our distance. When he arrived at his room, he jammed his key card into the receiver and attempted to squeeze his large frame in between the door and the doorframe.

By this time, Lewis and I were at the door behind him, as he attempted to push us out the door. When I peered into the room, I saw Christine lying on the bed. The mayor gave a forceful push and slammed the door. I looked at Lewis. "Did you see what I saw?"

Lewis replied, "Yeah, I saw Christine on the bed."

We walked away from Mayor Kilpatrick's room, laughing as usual.

"There are some occasions when a man must tell half his secrets,
in order to conceal the rest."
*Lord Philip Dormer Stanhope Chesterfield*

By early afternoon Lewis and I were in our room discussing how the mayor attempted to keep this clandestine relationship with Christine from us. Lewis then began to share with me how he should have been fired from the Detroit Police Department. He talked about how he had retained an expensive lawyer and avoided jail time. Without going into details, he explained that he had been negligent off duty, but his attorney got him off. He then expressed how Kilpatrick had resurrected his career and given him credibility. Finally Lewis said, "I will do anything for Kwame." He had an eerie look on his face as he said that.

There was a knock at our door. It was Kilpatrick and his father. I immediately said, "Mr. Mayor, you should not be walking around the hotel by yourself."

"Yeah, I know," he acknowledged, still dressed in his gym clothes. "Come on. We're going to a formal wear store."

I grabbed my firearm and identification and called Louis on my cell phone. While walking to the elevator, the mayor asked Lewis, "Where are you going?"

"With you to the store."

"Kev, you can't go with me dressed like that. Go back to the room." (Lewis was dressed in torn gym shorts and an oversized tank top.)

The mayor, his father, and I went to a men's store not far from the hotel. The mayor picked out some black onyx and diamond cufflinks. He wanted my approval and asked if I liked them.

"They're sharp, very classy," I said.

We left the store and stopped at a pharmacy. When we arrived there, the mayor said, "Give me some room, Walt," as he fanned his elbows. I stepped away from the mayor and his father to give them some privacy; however I continued to watch him from a distance. The mayor picked up some prophylactics and rushed to the counter. I met up with him at the front of the store. We left the drugstore and returned to the hotel. I escorted the mayor to his room. During the walk, he bragged about how good he would look that night.

Upon returning to my room, Lewis had a look of resentment on his face and acted standoffish. I attempted to smooth things over and told Lewis he had missed nothing.

At 7:45 p.m., Lewis and I arrived at the mayor's room. A few minutes later, he opened the door and invited us inside. I looked for Christine, but she was not there. The mayor was still getting dressed and asked for assistance with his new cufflinks. When he finished dressing, he took a few minutes to admire himself in the mirror. He secured his diamond stud in his ear. "Walt, how do I look?"

"Mr. Mayor, you look like a million bucks." (For some reason the mayor always turned to me for approval.)

Down in the lobby, we observed a large number of people in formal attire. Christine Beatty and Amy Malone, along with other appointees, met us there. I caught the mayor making goo-goo eyes at Christine, even though Carlita's watchdog was present. Kilpatrick told his appointees, "We will all ride together in the limo to the awards dinner."

Upon arrival at the convention center, we entered the ballroom for the Congressional Black Caucus Foundation's awards banquet.

The room was very large and decorated beautifully. There were colorful balloons, candles, fresh flowers and freshly pressed tablecloths on each table. The overall presentation was very professional; it appeared that no expense had been spared. There were hundreds, if not a thousand, people in attendance.

Lewis and I, dressed appropriately in tuxedos and black bowties, escorted Kilpatrick to his table. We stood in the background, along with the EPU for Mayor Anthony of Washington, D.C. The unit was very professional and cordial. Commander Thompson talked about how his unit was stretched thin because of covering all the dignitaries. I continued to watch how cozy the mayor and Christine looked, sitting together as a couple.

At 9:45 p.m., Kilpatrick decided it was time to go, and Louis drove him, Lewis, and me back to the hotel. The mayor said he wanted to go to a different nightclub, and I asked Louis if he knew where Club Nairobi was located. He said he knew exactly where it was.

"Let's change clothes," the mayor said. "Be at my room no later than 10:45 p.m." After escorting him to his room, we rushed to our room and switched out of our tuxedos.

Lewis and I were standing by the mayor's room at 10:35 p.m. Within six minutes, he exited his room, dressed in shirt and slacks. We took the elevator to the lobby and eased into the limo. As we pulled up to the front of the club, Lewis quickly left the limo, and I immediately followed. I thought his action was rather odd, before he eagerly stated, "I'll go in and talk to the manager."

I replied, "Okay, go see if they will accommodate the mayor."

Lewis returned, and we escorted Kilpatrick into the club. Although the club had multiple floors separated by stairs, a security officer posted at every entrance/exit allowed Kilpatrick to move unrestricted from floor to floor. On one level, there were chairs surrounding the dance floor. The mayor turned to us and said, "Y'all give me some room. I mean some room," as he threw his elbows violently outward.

I explained to Lewis that we needed to be on opposite sides of the mayor, letting him move throughout the club but remaining within striking distance.

Kilpatrick walked around the club, mingling with the women. I saw him dancing with three women on three separate occasions. After he completed his third dance, he walked toward the stairs. I signaled for Lewis to move ahead of the mayor, before he entered the doorway. Lewis did an excellent job in anticipating the mayor's next move.

We walked upstairs, and the mayor moved around as he started to mingle again. On this particular floor there were sofas and large chairs that were occupied by men and women. The mayor located an empty chair and sat down. The waitress asked the mayor if he wanted to order a drink. He requested top-shelf cognac, straight up.

After the mayor finished his drink, he walked toward the stairs. We went up another flight to a large bar, somewhat near the door. Kilpatrick walked over to a woman, maybe in her early twenties, and engaged in conversation for awhile. She was wearing a short white and multi-colored dress. With very fair complexion and long, curly, black hair, she appeared to be of mixed ethnicity, perhaps African American and Asian.

After a long conversation with her, the mayor headed for the stairs. We walked downstairs where the mayor stood around for awhile and then said to me, "Let's go!" I signaled Lewis, and we left the club. I made sure I thanked security for their accommodation.

We walked to the limo, and Lewis and the mayor entered the back seat. I entered the front passenger side and told Louis to hold on before he pulled away. I looked back into the limo and asked the mayor if he was ready.

Lewis replied, "Hold on, Walt!" He exited the limo and assisted the young mixed-race woman from the bar into the limo. I looked back and saw that she was sitting next to the mayor with his arm around her. There in front of the Club Nairobi, a man from another limo walked over. He was standing three feet away, as he said something to Louis who had his window down.

Louis answered the man, who moved closer and tried to stick his head in the window. I told Louis to close his window. He was moving in slow motion, and I yelled, "Close the window now!"

He closed the window before the man came any closer. Lewis yelled, "Walt, let's go!" I told Louis to head back to the hotel. When I peeked back at the mayor, he still had his arm around the woman and was whispering in her ear.

When we arrived back at the hotel, I opened the mayor's door. He stepped out and said, "Let's go, Walt."

I looked back at the limo and said, "Mr. Mayor, what about Kevin?"

He said with a grin on his face, "Awww, don't worry about Kev. He'll come inside in a minute."

The mayor and I walked through the lobby and entered the elevator. I pushed the button for the 12th Floor, and he pushed the 6th Floor button. I asked the mayor if he was going to the 6th Floor and he replied, "Yes." The elevator stopped, we stepped off and turned to the left. We walked a very short distance, and the mayor stopped at a room on the right. He said, "Walt, I'm done for the night. You can go now." He opened the door with his key card, stepped inside and closed the door.

I stood there for a couple of minutes, trying to figure out what was going on. I knew the mayor's room was on the 12th Floor, so what was he doing in a room on the sixth?

I walked back to the elevator and looked down into the atrium. I saw Lewis walking through the lobby with the young woman on his arm. He had an exaggerated walk, as he swung his arms high. He really drew attention to himself. He and the woman entered the elevator. It stopped at the 6th Floor, and they both stepped off. Lewis yelled, "Hey, Walt, I'll be back."

I watched Lewis walk the woman to the same room that the mayor had entered. When she stepped inside, he came back to me. "What in the hell is going on?" I asked.

"Man, you know the mayor is doing his thang," as he laughed. We continued to stand at the elevator and look down into the atrium. Two women in their hotel window that faced the atrium were desperately trying to get our attention. Lewis said, "Let's go see what they want, Walt. Come on."

Their room appeared to be directly across from the mayor's room. While walking the very short distance in the hallway, we were approached by an African American man. "Hey, it's the guys from Detroit," he shouted. "That's where I'm from." He had a woman with him dressed in a white jeans jacket and pants. She appeared to be very intoxicated, mumbling that she had to urinate.

As I examined her more closely, I recognized her as one of the actresses from the movie, "Set It Off." She whimpered, as urine began to run down her legs. She attempted to run, while stumbling from wall to wall down the hallway. The man quickly said, "I got to go. I have the room key." He started running to the room.

As we walked down the hall, the females who had been in the window were now standing in the doorway. We engaged in dialogue with them and learned they were from St. Louis. They wanted to party in their room, and Lewis was all for it. I told them I had business to take care of and left.

I returned to my room and began to prep my clothing for the next day. Lewis arrived at our room 10 minutes later and said, "The mayor will call in 30 minutes and have us throw that freak out the room." I went to bed, and the mayor never called our room.

I received a 6:30 a.m. wake-up call and proceeded to do my morning workout. I showered, dressed, and contacted Louis at the limo. He said he was outside and in position. After Lewis was dressed and ready, we went down to the sixth floor lounge for the continental breakfast. After we ate, Lewis fixed a plate with donuts and fresh fruit for the mayor.

At 7:45 a.m., Lewis and I were standing outside the mayor's room. We heard him and a woman laughing and talking. I turn to Lewis and said, "That chick stayed all night."

Then we heard the shower running. "He's just getting into the shower," I said. "He's going to be late for his 8:30 appointment."

Suddenly the door opened and the mayor stepped out quickly, closing the door behind him. He was fully dressed in his suit and gators. Lewis handed the plate of food to the mayor, and he ate only the fruit. We entered the elevator and headed for the limo. The mayor made his appointment on time, and we returned to the hotel to collect our luggage. We left Washington, DC and arrived in Detroit that afternoon.

> "We're all borne brave, trusting, and greedy,
> and most of us remain greedy."
> *Mignon Mc Laughlin*

While walking through the Northwest Airlines Terminal, I was approached by a Wayne County deputy sheriff. He stepped up to me closely and almost whispered, "I know you know about the party at the Manoogian Mansion."

I looked at the deputy, puzzled, and asked, "What party? What are you referring to?"

"Hey, take a look at Al Jackson's paycheck," he said.

"Al's check?"

"Be careful with Kwame. The Feds are watching him." The deputy walked away, leaving me confused about all that he had said. I couldn't wait to get back to the office and inquire about the party and Jackson's paycheck.

When arrived at the mayor's office, I pulled Lewis to the side. "What is this party at the Manoogian Mansion all about?"

His face flushed red, and he replied in an angry tone, "There was no party. Don't ever mention it again."

I thought he was trying to protect somebody. I started asking other officer that I trusted about the party. That was when I collected bits and pieces of a rumor about Carlita arriving unexpectedly at the party and assaulting one of the strippers.

I also had a private conversation with Officer Regina Tucker. I asked her why someone would ask me to inquire about Jackson's paycheck. Tucker, who was the timekeeper, pulled me to the rear of the office. She looked around to make sure no one else was present. She then said that the overtime she had received from Jackson was fraudulent. Jackson would contact her by phone and verbally submit his overtime. Even though he was the commanding officer of the unit, he was still required to turn in an overtime sheet.

"Okay, that's nothing to be clandestine about," I responded.

"You don't understand," Tucker continued. "I am scared to death! Officer Jackson has been calling in with 80 to 105 hours of overtime per pay period. I have to fill out his overtime sheet. I'm the timekeeper. I could be held responsible."

I advised Tucker to document or record the conversations whenever Jackson called on Sunday. She should keep a notebook, documenting all her dealings with Jackson. I explained to Tucker that later if she is subpoenaed, her notebook would become a legal document.

When I learned that the information about Jackson's paycheck was reliable, it lent credibility to the Manoogian party and to Kilpatrick being under surveillance by the Feds. According to the local newspaper, the wild Manoogian party was believed to have occurred Wednesday, September 4, 2002.

I also read that the DC mayor's security had denied any future late-evening courtesy protection for Mayor Kilpatrick; instead, it would provide only DC police protection while he was conducting official business there. The article reported how the Detroit mayor had partied at an "off-limit" establishment; therefore, DC police after-hours protection was terminated. Commander Thompson arrived at his decision because he felt that the late evening partying, on the part of Mayor Kilpatrick, would leave his department's officers stretched too thin and might result in an incident at one of the clubs.

# Chapter 8

# Philandering

*"If the camel once gets his nose in a tent,
his body will soon follow."*
*Saudi Arabian proverb*

In June 2002, I traveled to Chicago with the mayor. He had been asked to be the keynote speaker for the 88th Annual Awards and Installation Banquet for the Cook County Bar Association.

The trip was originally listed for Officer Lewis to serve as his security officer, but the mayor requested me instead. The mayor's secretary said, "Hey, Walt, the mayor must like you! He scratched his boy Kevin and requested that you travel with him instead!" I immediately started thinking how fatigued I was going to be, because I was currently working a 24-hour shift.

The next day I drove home, showered and dressed, packed my bags, and ate breakfast. I left my home headed for Detroit Metro Airport. Deputy Chief Ronald Fleming and Officer Gerald King had gone ahead to Chicago to complete the advance, because I was traveling without a security partner.

When we arrived at Chicago's Midway Airport, we were picked up by a chauffeured limo. Fleming and King met us at the hotel. We received our room keys and completed a walkthrough of the location. Fleming explained how he wanted to train King on how to do out-of-town advance work. Shortly thereafter they returned to Detroit.

I escorted Kilpatrick to his room, and he said he would call me when he was ready. I walked next door to my room and relaxed. At 6:45 p.m., the mayor called. I escorted him to the ballroom which was full of lawyers and judges eager to hear him speak. He gave an excellent speech and ended with an analogy of a newspaper and a picture of Earth. He told that one day, when he was a Michigan state representative, he went home from work and retired to the couch, where his kids joined him. "Come on, Daddy, let's go play. Come on! Let's go outside."

Kilpatrick said he saw a newspaper lying on the floor with a huge picture of Earth. He picked up the newspaper and tore it into many small pieces. He then told his kids, "If y'all can put that newspaper back together again, we'll go outside and play!"

He stretched back out on the couch and thought to himself, I've got them now. He continued watching television. Ten minutes later the kids said they were finished. The mayor quickly sat up, looked at the newspaper, and saw that it had been reassembled correctly with the whole Earth intact. He thought his kids were geniuses!

The mayor asked his boys, "How did y'all do that?"

Both of his sons answered, "Daddy, there are pictures of kids on the back page. So when we put the kids together, the whole world fell into place."

The bar association members jumped to their feet and applauded non-stop. The mayor left the stage and was met by a swarm of lawyers and judges who stated they want to become a mayor. Kilpatrick shook almost every person's hand in the room. When we left the banquet, he said he wanted to meet up with some of his friends from FAMU (Florida A&M University).

We walked a couple of blocks from the hotel to a bar/lounge. We joined his friends in a large, half-moon-shaped booth. Two women and one man hugged and shook hands with the mayor. He introduced his college friends to me. One of the ladies maintained heavy eye contact with me when she shook my hand. The ladies were dressed casually in tight-fitting jeans and were fairly attractive.

The mayor asked if I wanted to sit with his friends and have a drink. I was still on duty, so I declined the offer and told the mayor that I preferred to stand. I actually was afraid I would have fallen asleep if I sat down. "Hey, Walt, do your thang," he said.

The mayor ordered top-shelf cognac and shared some laughs with his friends. He then pointed at me and started laughing. "Look at Walt, y'all! He's sleepy because he worked 24 hours yesterday."

I walked over to the bar where I saw an advertisement for Red Bull® energy drink. I asked the bartender if it really worked. She swore by the drink and asked if I wanted one. "I'll try anything at this point." I said.

She poured Red Bull over ice and slid it over to me. I stood at the bar and examined the drink, before consuming it all at once. I then returned to the booth and stood behind it. Within a short amount of time, I began to feel energized.

The mayor knocked off a couple more drinks with his college buddies and advised me that he was ready to leave. He pulled out the City of Detroit credit card and told his friends he was picking up the tab. As we were leaving the bar, I thanked the bartender for rescuing me from fatigue.

Outside, the mayor and his friends talked and at times whispered. The mayor was standing approximately seven feet away, when he called out to me, "Hey, Walt."

"Yes, Mr. Mayor! Do you need something?"

"Hey, Walt, my girl likes you!"

I paused for a moment and responded, "I am flattered."

"The girls want to come back to the hotel and hang out with us," he continued.

I expressed to the mayor that if he wanted to take the women back to the hotel, it was his decision. "Mr. Mayor, I can't party with you, sir. I am working and I am married."

Mayor Kilpatrick laughed it off and said his goodbye, as the two women and the man entered their vehicle. As the car pulled away and turned the corner, the mayor's cell phone rang. He answered it and looked over at me, smiling. "Hey, Walt, the girls want to come to the room!"

I waved my hand at the mayor, indicating no. He told the person on the phone, "Naw, that's not going to happen. He's married."

The mayor put his cell phone back in his pocket, and we walked back to the hotel. He was very quiet and reserved. In the hotel elevator, he turned his back to me, not wanting to talk. I walked to the mayor's room in silence. He used his key card to unlock his door. Just as the mayor stepped inside his room, I asked, "Mr. Mayor, what time do you plan on eating breakfast?"

Mayor Kilpatrick did not turn around; he just slammed the door in my face. The door closed so hard that it shook the floor. I just stood there in shock, wondering what the hell was wrong with him. I entered my room, puzzled and disturbed by the mayor's behavior and actions. After thinking it over, it dawned on me: Kilpatrick was upset because I declined the girls' offer to visit our rooms.

The flight home was uneventful; however, once we returned home, there was more evidence of the mayor's philandering ways.

One summer evening while working a crew with Officer Nelthrope, we had to escort the mayor to a barbershop, located just a few blocks from his residence on the west side of the city. This was before the family moved into the Manoogian Mansion. While en route to the shop, the mayor was talking on his cell phone. "Hey, I'll meet you over there. Yeah, meet me. You know the shop." He disconnected and said, "Hey, Walt, I want you to meet this Jamaican friend of mine. Tell me how she looks and how you like her."

As we approached the barbershop, we had to pull into an empty parking lot, so that he could make another phone call prior to arriving at the shop. We waited there at least 10 minutes before a woman pulled up next to our car in a dark Honda Civic or Prelude. The mayor lowered his window and said, "Follow us." He told Nelthrope to drive to the shop.

She followed us, and we both pulled into the parking lot. The mayor and the woman stepped out of their respective vehicles. I made sure to observe the woman's features in order to respond to the mayor's question about her looks. She was an attractive woman with long, spirally curled, black hair. She was neatly dressed with a very short skirt accentuating her long legs. She and the mayor exchanged words, hugged, and kissed on the lips. Immediately I looked around to see if anyone was watching. The kiss took me by surprise, and I wanted to know if there were any witnesses. I was shocked that he showed so much affection to this woman in public and in such close proximity to his residence.

We all walked into the shop where the mayor extended brief greetings to the barber, and then the mayor and the woman entered a private room located at the back of the shop. He did not allow any of us to follow them into the room.

My partner and I waited near the front door. While the mayor was in the back room, we noticed Carlita's vehicle pass the shop. Nelthrope asked me if he should inform the mayor. I knew she must have seen the mayor's vehicle and wondered if she would double back. No sense in alarming the mayor unnecessarily. However, it certainly gave us cause for alarm, just imagining her finding out that he was in the private room with another woman. Fortunately, she didn't stop or come to the shop.

After 30 minutes, the mayor and the woman emerged from the private room. As always, he was composed, calm and cool, and gave the impression that nothing but business had gone on while they were in the room. I often saw this same expression on his face after his private "meetings" with Christine Beatty.

By January 2003, I was beginning to think this was not the unit for me. Not only did I have to witness the mayor's activities with Christine Beatty, but I also knew that he met with other women.

The Detroit Auto Show 2003 was fast approaching. Officer Raymond Green and I escorted the mayor and his wife to the ribbon-cutting ceremony. It was a black tie affair and, as always, we were running late. Mayor Kilpatrick almost missed the ceremony. We rushed in as the other dignitaries watched in dismay.

The mayor participated in the ceremony and then walked around the event with his wife looking at the new cars on display. It was a grand gala with many celebrities and other high-ranking officials on hand. After the mayor looked at the vehicles and completed the obligatory pleasantries, we moved on to the next event.

The "firehouse" in downtown Detroit hosted an after-party for various dignitaries that attended the auto show. Unfortunately, the mayor and his wife had a big argument as we left the party. Carlita was not invited to the next event, and she displayed considerable frustration. She could not understand why she couldn't accompany her husband to the party at the Omni Hotel. He left her at the curb with her security detail and proceeded to attend the Omni event without her.

The entire time he attended various parties, his appointees, Phil Mason and Jerome Fisher, were part of his entourage. During the Omni Hotel party, the mayor and Mason made arrangements for a private meeting later at the Renaissance Hotel. It wasn't until much later that I realized that this private meeting was with two women, one of whom was a member of his office staff.

We left the Omni and proceeded to a downtown nightclub, where the mayor hosted his own party. He had called ahead of us to make sure the women he planned to meet later were going to attend his small party. Upon arriving there, food and drinks were set up to receive the mayor and his entourage. Many of his guests were already in attendance. He met Bobby Ferguson at the front door. It was very obvious that Ferguson was very intoxicated and needed the assistance of his wife.

The party was located in a basement room. I escorted the mayor, Mason, and Fisher down the stairs, and they all took seats at a vacant table. Other guests began to arrive, and the mayor greeted them at the door. A glass partition allowed me to monitor the mayor from a distance. The security team was not allowed to be in the same room as the mayor; he wanted us to wait for him in the hallway.

Ferguson staggered into the hall and began to ramble in a drunken slur about something that I could not understand. Next, his wife came out, and Ferguson demanded that I escort her to the restroom. I told him that escorting his wife was not my job. I was there for the mayor's security. He started yelling profanities to me, as his wife walked to the restroom. He yelled at me the entire time she was in the restroom. When she returned, she had to calm him down. I just simply ignored him and continued to monitor the mayor.

I noticed that while all this was going on, Jackson and Lewis were escorting two more guests down the stairs. One of the women looked very familiar. As they came closer, I recognized her as an actress in the movie "Coming to America." They entered the party and engaged in conversion with the mayor. He called me over to his table. He wanted to make sure that if the actress ever came into his office, I would not stop her from seeing him. He most certainly was taken by her presence and beauty, as he could not stop staring at her. I returned to my post and shared the conversation with my partner.

At that point, a General Motors executive came down the stairs. He looked around and said to his wife before entering the room, "Boy, this reminds me of a speakeasy" (a term frequently used for an illegal nightclub). By then, the room was getting rather full of people, making their obligatory stop to see the mayor.

The next two people to arrive were Stacey Turner, a mayoral office staff member, and the other woman, whom I had seen often at past functions sponsored by the mayor. When they reached the entrance of the doorway, the mayor turned in his seat facing Ms. Turner and bit his lip. His face displayed the look of a man who saw a woman that he wanted to seduce. His face could not hide the lust and attraction that he had for this woman. He stood up, walked over to the doorway, and took her hand. He escorted the two women to his table, where they shared food and alcoholic beverages.

The party continued until after midnight. The mayor was pleased that the owner of the club was able to accommodate his party on short notice.

Officer Green and I received another surprise: we were going to yet another party at that late hour. We chauffeured the mayor and his entourage to the Renaissance Hotel. It was a very cold night.

After entering the hotel, we took the elevator to the 2nd Floor lobby; my partner parked the vehicle. We met Tim Dugan, the hotel security director on duty. Fisher asked him for the room keys. The security director went to the computer and returned with two plastic key cards and handed them to Fisher. He then turned to the mayor and Mason and gave them each a key. Fisher left the hotel, stating he had a "hot date" waiting for him!

The mayor went to the elevators still dressed in his tuxedo from the black tie affair and pushed the elevator button for the 40th Floor. When the doors opened, I asked the mayor which rooms we were going to, and he dismissed my question by motioning his hand to keep walking. Down the hallway I asked him again for the room number. His response was "Walt, man, you don't need to know about this. Go back downstairs."

I reminded him that my job was to protect him at all times and that I need to know which room he would be occupying. Once again his response was, "Don't worry about it. Go back downstairs."

I returned to the 2nd Floor lobby. There, I was able to sit where I could monitor who entered and exited the elevator. At this point, my partner arrived and seemed confused, because I was sitting without the mayor. "Where's the mayor?"

I told him that he was somewhere on the 40th Floor and that he had demanded that I leave. We both sat down and continued watching the elevators.

Stacey Turner and her friend arrived. They too were puzzled that the mayor was not with his security officers. "Is he upstairs?" she asked, smiling as she pointed her finger upward.

"Yes," I responded.

The women then entered the elevators. By that time, my partner and I figured it was going to be a long night. I was actually happy to have a chance to rest my feet. My new tuxedo shoes were not broken in and caused some discomfort. My partner took his winter coat off and sat in a comfortable chair next to me.

After a couple of hours, the mayor and Mason exited the elevator walking at a very fast pace. I remember chuckling to myself the way their coats were swinging; they looked like Batman and Robin. I directed my partner to hurry out to the car and start it. I didn't want the mayor to arrive at the car before my partner did.

I caught up with the mayor and escorted him out of the hotel. He requested that we drop off Mason at his Indian Village home and then proceed to Manoogian.

> "A mistress should be like a little country retreat near a little town,
> not to dwell in constantly but only for a night and away."
> *William Wycherley*

It was a winter evening, and my crew was responsible for escorting the mayor and his wife to Birmingham to a late evening movie, "Deliver us from Eva," staring LL Cool J and Gabrielle Union. My partner was responsible for picking up popcorn and drinks for them. The theatre was packed, forcing us to sit separately from the Kilpatricks.

When the movie ended, we took them by way of Starbuck's and then to the mansion. We arrived there, and the mayor announced that he was done for the night, indicating that we are to retire the vehicles and stay on watch at the home. Our typical routine also involved removing our police radios, batons, ear pieces, and changing into more relaxed or comfortable clothing, a nice break from spending the evening sitting in a suit.

The night didn't remain quiet for long. Shortly after we arrived, Officer Green received an emergency call from his wife and needed to go home immediately. The mansion was then left for Officer Brian Washington and me to guard, and I alerted the mayor that just two of us would be working the EPU for the night.

Unfortunately, the situation at Green's house involved a man who had been shot and randomly stopped at Green's house for help. His wife didn't open the door, but she called the police department. Green's concern was for the safety of his family.

I was relaxed and watching the security monitors and my partner was on the computer in another room. Close to the midnight, I heard the mayor come down the stairs. He came into the security office. I noticed that he was dressed in blue jeans, a leather jacket, and large hat that partially covered his face. He grabbed the keys to the Cadillac and turned to me, "Walt, let's go." This was very unusual, because we normally met him in the garage with the car started and ready to go.

I said, "Just me?"

"Yeah, just you. Let's go." He went upstairs, and I went to get my partner, Officer Washington, and let him know that I had to go solo with the mayor. I had to move quickly to catch up to him. I grabbed my radio and equipment and put them on my belt as I was running up the stairs.

By the time I reached the garage, the mayor had started the car and was seated in the front passenger seat. The gate was open, ready for us to leave. I pulled out and asked the mayor where we were going.

"Just drive. Take me to Jefferson." It was a very cold and windy night, and the ground was snow covered. I drove toward McArthur Bridge, also known as Belle Isle Bridge, located off Jefferson Avenue. I was perplexed about this outing, because it was completely outside of our normal protocol. He never sat in the front seat with the driver, nor did he ever grab the keys and open the security gate. My concern was for my partner who was left to secure the Manoogian Mansion alone. This was a compromise of his security and the Kilpatrick family's safety, as Mrs. Kilpatrick was at home with the children.

I continued to inquire about our destination, and the mayor told me only when and where to turn. He didn't specify whom he was going to meet or give details of his plans once he arrived at the location. Just past the turn-off for McArthur Bridge, there is a Wendy's on Jefferson. The mayor told me to turn onto that street and drive slowly. I thought this was odd. Why so secretive just to go out for something to eat?

However, I soon realized we were not going into the restaurant. Adjacent to this location was an apartment complex. "Slow down!" he said. I had to pass the driveway that led to the apartment complex parking lot and make a U-turn, returning to the private driveway. A vehicle with its high beams on approached us. I thought this must be the person or people we were supposed to meet.

I asked the mayor if he was familiar with that vehicle, and he said, "No." By that time, my adrenaline was kicking in, my heart was racing, and I began to prepare myself for a potential threat. Then the car simply drove past us, completely ignoring us.

I was glad to see the car drive on by, yet I remained perplexed as to why we were in the driveway. Suddenly a woman dressed in a full-length black mink coat walked up to the security arm that blocked us at the driveway. She reached into her pocket to remove the security gate key so that the arm would lift and we could pull through. Just as she reached into her pocket, a gust of wind blew her coat open. It was very easy to see that she was not dressed; she was completely naked. The mayor realized I saw the same thing as he did, and his response was to turn to me and chuckle. My silent response was here we go again.

With the security arm lifted, I was instructed to pull into a dark corner located at the back of the parking lot. The mayor exited the vehicle and greeted the woman, whom I never seen before. I quickly exited the car and asked the mayor which apartment he would be visiting. He responded "Don't worry about it. Stay in the car." He kissed the woman on the lips and walked away arm in arm. I watched as they entered the apartment building. This woman was a stranger to me, someone I had never seen at the mayor's office, functions, or outings, and she wasn't one of his relatives, to the best of my knowledge.

I sat in the car for at least an hour. During that time, I informed my partner of my location and what had transpired. I told him that I was on stand-by in the vehicle as ordered by the mayor. I was uncomfortable waiting in the car and felt the need to continue to scan the parking lot for safety. I also tried to determine which direction the mayor might use when he exited the building.

Most of my time was spent listening to the police department's district radio. I always feared in the back of my mind that one day, one of the mayor's women would scream rape. I did not want to be implicated and accused as an accessory to his misdeed.

When the mayor returned to the vehicle, he did not look at me, and we drove silently back to the mansion. After he was secured inside the mansion, I returned to the security office. Officer Washington was operating the control center and wanted the play-by-play on the mayor's visit. I simply told him it was the same old song with a different beat.

In March 2003, the mayor was expected to attend a fundraiser in Washington, D.C. in support of his mother. Upon arriving at the airport there, we were met at the curb by James "Jimmy" Wilkinson, one of the mayor's appointees. We carried our luggage and met Louis the limo driver at the curb. He was the same limo driver we had on the September 2002 Washington trip.

The mayor and I checked into the hotel and dropped off our luggage in our respective rooms. We met Detective Neeley of the Washington EPU in the hotel lobby; she was assigned to Mayor Kilpatrick for the two-day visit. Kilpatrick spoke with his mother on his cell, and she asked him to make reservations for dinner. Neeley followed our limo in her unmarked unit.

At the restaurant, Kilpatrick asked that I go inside and get a table for 10 people. I spoke with the assistant general manager, Tony Rizetti. I identified myself and my law enforcement agency and asked if he could accommodate Mayor Kilpatrick and nine guests. He was more than happy to assist and asked that I give him a moment to set up a large table. When he was ready for us, he gave me the signal. I returned to the limo and escorted Kilpatrick into the restaurant. The mayor was pleased with the table. "That's what I'm talking about, Walt. You know how to get things done."

Minutes later, Congresswoman Kilpatrick arrived with a host of people. Sharply dressed in one of her signature St. John's outfits, she was cordial, as we exchanged pleasantries. The mayor requested that I join the group for dinner. I declined his offer and stood in the background with Neeley.

After the mayor and his guests were situated for dinner, Neeley went across the street to the MCI Center, the location of the fundraiser. She spoke with security and arranged to have the Congresswoman Kilpatrick, Mayor Kilpatrick, and guests escorted to their private suite.

Detective Neeley returned to the restaurant and advised me that everything was set up for the mayor and guests. Congresswoman Kilpatrick looked at her watch and suggested that everyone prepare to leave. The mayor presented his City of Detroit credit card and paid for dinner.

We walked over to the MCI Center to the congresswoman's reserved suite. I observed that the Washington Wizards were hosting the Detroit Pistons. I watched as guests walked into the suite and handed envelopes to the congresswoman. I gathered that they contained donations to her fundraiser.

Detective Neeley and I stood in the rear of the suite, sampling some of the finger foods; we were hungry, as we had not eaten at the restaurant. Mayor Kilpatrick walked over and said, "What are y'all doing? Walt, you know there's no fraternizing." He grinned and walked away, occasionally looking over his shoulder at us. I looked at Detective Neeley and shook my head. "See what I have to put up with." She just laughed it off.

After the game ended, the mayor said we were going to a club. He asked if I was taking Neeley back to my room. I quickly responded, "No. Mr. Mayor, we are professionals."

I called Louis the limo driver and gave him the name of the club. Upon leaving the MCI Center, the mayor asked some of the guests to ride with us. We arrived at the club/lounge, and there was a long line of people waiting to enter. Kilpatrick asked me to see if they could accommodate him and his guests. I walked past the long line of people, approached the doorman, and identified myself. I explained that Mayor Kilpatrick and seven guests would like to visit the club. I asked him if he could accommodate them. He asked me to give him a few minutes and left. When he returned, he said, "I have a table for them now."

I escorted the mayor and his guests into the club. Detective Neeley had advised me before we left the MCI Center that she would wait outside any club.

Inside, the doorman gave the mayor a large booth in his own section with his own waitress. I positioned myself at a table across from the booth. The mayor and his party ordered drinks and seemed to have a good time.

Twenty minutes later, two women walked into the club and entered the mayor's area. He signaled to me that they were okay. One woman sat at the mayor's table, and the other one sat at my table. She was attractive and introduced herself. She said she was tired and that it had been a long day. She asked if I was with the mayor and what my connection was to him.

When I explained that I provided security, Mayor Kilpatrick looked at the woman and then back at me. He then gave me an angry face. I immediately got up and walked to the entrance of his section. I thought, this man has a serious problem.

We left the club at approximately 12:30 a.m. and returned to the Westin Grand Hotel. I escorted the mayor to his room. He told me to be ready at 4:30 a.m., because he was scheduled to be on C-Span at 5:00 a.m.

I received a wake-up call at 3:00 a.m. and completed my morning exercise routine. I called Louis to find out if he was ready.

By 4:15 a.m., I was standing at the mayor's door with my carry-on luggage and the morning newspaper.

Fifteen minutes later, Mayor Kilpatrick exited his room with his luggage and adjusted his tie. Down in the lobby, we waited for Jimmy Wilkins. The mayor looked at his watch. "Where in the hell is he?"

At 4:40 a.m., Mayor Kilpatrick and I enter the limo, headed for the C-Span Building. Twelve minutes later, we entered the building, walking very fast, and met Congresswoman Kilpatrick. The C-Span engineer placed a microphone on her and on the mayor. I sat in a separate room with a television monitor and with my Skypager® I paged everyone in the unit that the mayor and congresswoman were on C-Span.

When the interview was over, the mayor got on his cell phone. I heard him tell Wilkins, "You better have your ass at the airport."

The limo dropped us off at Reagan National Airport, and there was Jimmy Wilkins standing outside, hung over from the night before. Just as the mayor exited the limo, he pointed at Wilkins. "Where in the hell were you? You get so damn drunk that you couldn't make the interview! The only reason your ass came to DC was for the interview! Jimmy, that's bullshit." The mayor walked away very angry.

We rushed into the terminal and checked in with security. The airport police escorted us to the departure gate. We left DC and arrived in Detroit by 8:00 a.m.

Until that trip, I had never seen a mayor's appointee miss a significant event in the previous administration and, before this one, not in Kilpatrick's. However, more and more I was feeling that there were improper activities in the administration as well as in the EPU. The most disturbing incident for me occurred sometime during the spring of 2003.

One morning as Officer Marvin Koch and I began our shift, we followed routine and checked the vehicles, making sure they had gas and were clean and ready to go. That particular morning, he checked the SUV, and I took the Cadillac. While he was inspecting the SUV, he called to me, "Walt! Get over here!"

He told me to look in the back seat. I was surprised by what I saw: plates of dried up food, silverware, and what appeared to be empty champagne bottles and glasses. "Wow, the mayor must have had a party last night!" I said. I told him to clean it up and get going. He quickly said, "No, look on the floor between the seats!"

That's when I noticed light blue women's panties. I took the pen out of my pocket, breaking into my police investigative mode, and lifted the panties up. I noticed how small they were and that they were ripped along one side. I tossed them back on the floor.

"Well, I don't think he partied with his wife," I commented. "The first lady isn't that small!"

We just looked at each other, trying not to laugh. We had to get the cars cleaned. We followed each other to the car wash that serviced the mayor's vehicles. We pulled in line so that the SUV would get cleaned first. I cleaned out the plates and glasses and noticed that the underwear was missing. "What happened to the panties?"

"I threw them away," he responded.

The next day I was back on shift at the mansion, and the mayor planned to spend a casual day. As Nelthrope and I prepared to leave with the mayor, he stopped us and said, "Wait, Koch has a package for me. We need to wait a minute."

The mayor was very laid-back about it, started shooting the basketball in the back, and casually looked our way from time to time in anticipation of Koch's arrival. Koch wasn't on duty that morning, so I was curious about his arrival with a package. I didn't give it much thought, however; it could have been anything from food to something Kilpatrick told him to pick up. But coming over on his off day, it must have been important.

Officer Koch walked up the driveway and met the mayor just outside of the garage. He gave me a surprised look; I don't think he expected me to be on duty. Koch reached in his pocket and gave the mayor a plastic grocery bag that had been rolled up and tied together. The mayor's attention was directly on Koch, not on us. With a slight smile on his face, he tucked the package in his breast pocket, shot a few more baskets, and turned toward the house.

Once the mayor was in the mansion, my curiosity got the best of me. I asked Koch what was in the bag. He walked close to me and looked over at Nelthrope, while pulling me aside. He leaned close to my ear and said, "It was the panties from the back of the car! The mayor wanted them back."

I was shocked. "What? I thought you threw them out. How did he find out?"

"I told him."

"What is he going to do with them?"

We both tried to laugh it off. It was very uncomfortable for me, and I tried to use humor to break the stress.

Koch just responded with, "You know he gets out at night." This must have been one of those nights when he took the car out at night by himself to do whatever. It wasn't his first time to sneak out and take off with one of his vehicles.

At this point I had had enough. The incident with the panties made me very, very uncomfortable. Although around "the guys," I tried to blow it off as a man just being a man, deep down I was dreadfully concerned. What if a woman had been forced to engage in a sexual act? What if the mayor had forced his way on the woman and ripped her panties? What if it didn't happen in the throes of passion? Who was this woman? Was she now a victim? Or was she just another one of the mayor's secret lovers?

Mrs. Kilpatrick is a healthy-sized woman, and the small woman's panties most likely did not belong to her. I have investigated these types of acts during my years at the precinct and as an investigator in Indiana. These unanswered questions did not set well with me. I wouldn't want that to happen to my wife, my sister, or any woman if it was against her will.

This situation bothered me for days. I had to stop myself from confronting the mayor, because I didn't think it would go over well with him. I had seen his anger toward others; he had a very thuggish persona once angered. I knew that if I confronted him, he would turn his wrath upon me.

My awareness of the many indiscretions against his wife, of officers bribing to pad overtime, of officers driving drunk on duty and drinking on duty became quite clear. Now I had to ponder the possibility of being implicated in a rape! Had I encouraged discarding the evidence? I'll never know. Wow, this really was the last straw! I had lost all respect for this mayor and his administration. I was embarrassed to be a part of it and to be seen with him. I felt it was time to leave but how far could I run? Do I go back the precinct, transfer to a different unit, or leave the department all together?

# PART 3

# *The Whistleblower Ordeal*

# Chapter 9

# Time to Leave

*"If your ship doesn't come in, swim out to it!"*
*Jonathan Winters*

The first awareness I had that I should get out of the Kilpatrick EPU was rather soon after I started. However, I wasn't exactly sure how to leave and where to go. I had to make a decision and, for the most part, I thought it would be best if I left the department altogether. I didn't want to give up my vested time or my hometown, yet I just couldn't see any other way out.

In May 2002, I traveled with the mayor to Las Vegas, NV and witnessed him juggle his trysts with Christine Beatty, spending time with his family, and doing business for the city. At the end of the trip, I spoke with a Las Vegas police officer assigned to the McCarran International Airport. He explained that the Las Vegas Metro Police Department was recruiting police officers for lateral entry, which meant that I could keep the seniority that I had in Detroit. It was very attractive, because the pay was more and I wouldn't have to start all over.

When I returned home, I had a long conversation with my wife. Although I didn't share with her the many details of what was happening in the EPU, she knew that I was very unhappy and wanted to leave. She was pregnant with our third child, and I didn't want to cause her undue stress. I pitched the idea of living in sunny Nevada and that I could move on in law enforcement without losing seniority. She was concerned about raising the kids there. I told her that there were nice communities just outside of Las Vegas that she would really like. With much thought and discussion, although I think she was a bit reluctant to leave Detroit and her family, she was very supportive in my decision to apply to the Las Vegas Police Department.

On September 27, 2002, I received my application. When I removed it from the mailbox, I knew I had a way out of Kwame Kilpatrick's Administration. I immediately completed the lengthy questionnaire and pre-employment polygraph booklet. Soon after I returned the packet, I received a call from Detective Vivian Springs. She was my background investigator and assisted me through the process. She explained that the written test would be in October. Upon passing the written exam, I would be issued a schedule for an oral/practical exam. The lateral-entry testing process was to be completed within five days.

I booked my flight and arrived in Las Vegas on October 14, 2002, picked up my rental car, and checked into my hotel. I stayed in my room except to eat, because I was there on business. The next day, I met Detective Springs at the police department.

In the exam room, there were approximately 15 officers from all over the United States. I was a little nervous just before I completed the written exam. I passed it and was scheduled for an oral/practical exam on October 16, 2002 at 01:00 p.m. The test administrator reminded everyone to be careful of what and how much they drank. He told about a candidate who came to his oral board hung over.

I returned to the hotel, purchased some carry-out Chinese food at the restaurant, and immediately went to my room.

On Wednesday, October 16, 2002, I drove back to the Las Vegas Police Department for the practical exam. I watched a video about a police call, and then I had to write a report, essay-style, about it. The report writing grade was mailed to me a week later, and I received 94 percent out of 100.

The last part of the process was the oral interview. Before I left the testing site, I spoke with Detective Springs. She said that when they call me, I had to be ready to have my physical and polygraph taken and make my move to Las Vegas.

Within two weeks of returning home, I received a phone call from Detective Springs. She delivered the bad news that there was a hiring freeze for the basic and lateral-entry academy. She stated that she understood I had spent a lot of time and money. Unfortunately her department was making these adjustments due to budget concerns.

I was devastated by the news and felt trapped in a corrupt system. I had to stay with the EPU and figure out how to play the game, "Survivor." I had to find the right alliances and continue to exist within the unit.

> "Wisdom consists of the anticipation of consequences."
> *Norman Cousins*

As the months passed, I continued to witness illegal activities by Jackson and Lewis. They were submitting false overtime documents (in excess of 80 to 100 hours on multiple occasions), drinking on the job, destroying police department property (a brand new Ford Crown Victoria), and offering me overtime pay for no work performed. I also witnessed Mayor Kilpatrick with a variety of women in assorted locations. Those meetings occurred while I was with him, on duty, in and out of town. With all this illegal and immoral activity taking place on a regular basis, I believed someone would end up going to prison. I refused to be implicated and wear an orange prison jumpsuit for anyone who is a criminal.

> "Frank (Frank Serpico), let's face it,
> who can trust a cop that won't take money?"
> *Tom Keough*

Kilpatrick, Jackson, and Lewis consistently tried to get me to participate in various activities that I knew were wrong, whether immoral or illegal, such as drinking on duty, but I refused to join in. Jackson once offered to give me overtime pay for work that I had not performed. He agreed to give me as much as I wanted, because, he said, I was the mayor's best guy. I thought back to the movie "Serpico" and refused the money, even though it would have made everyone feel more comfortable. This was basically a bribe from Jackson, and the mayor was aware of the offer.

Kilpatrick asked me on two different occasions if I needed more money. All crew chiefs on the detail were issued city vehicles through the mayor's office. Lewis continued to offer me a new Ford Crown Victoria, but I refused it and insisted that I keep my old Chevy

Lumina. It was in poor condition with no hub caps, but it was assigned from the city fleet.

Kilpatrick and Jackson continually tried to reel me in, but I refused to take the bait. On an out-of-town trip, the mayor attempted to set me up with one of his beautiful lady friends. When I refused to take her to my hotel room, the mayor became very angry at me.

The temptations became so great, and it was becoming more and more difficult to resist them. During each temptation, I could hear my mother saying, "Please don't fall for any snares that people will lay for you. People will set a trap for you, and then hold it over your head."

I often revisited in my mind the movie "Training Day," starring actors Denzel Washington and Ethan Hawk. The movie's main character, Detective Alonzo Harris, told Officer Jake Hoyt (while sitting in their black Monte Carlo, after killing Roger and stealing money hidden in the kitchen floor) "Sometimes you gotta have a little dirt on you for anybody to trust you."

Kilpatrick, Jackson, and Lewis tried their best to get some dirt on me. I always held close to my heart that I would not tarnish the badge by forsaking the public trust and compromising my integrity.

I stayed unsoiled, even while sharing the mayor's secrets with Officer Nelthrope, whom I had supervised him when he worked in the EPU. We became good friends and co-workers in 2002. I informed him that Lewis was planning to move him from my crew to the mansion. Lewis felt that Nelthrope would eventually begin to talk about the mayor's extramarital philandering. Lewis believed that Nelthrope could be minimized by not allowing him to go out with the mayor. I convinced Nelthrope to stay in the unit and become the best in-house security officer in the EPU. He was removed from the crew and placed in the mansion, and he took my advice.

He became the go-to guy for the unit and for the Kilpatricks. He mastered the mansion's security system and all its operations and was on a first-name basis with the interior decorator and maintenance personnel. He occasionally had to tell the hired workers that they were on the clock and needed to start working.

Nelthrope developed a favorable relationship with Carlita Kilpatrick too, and she valued his opinion. He was doing such an outstanding job that DC Fleming issued him a city vehicle and a cell phone. Lewis disapproved of the relationship between Officer Nelthrope and Carlita Kilpatrick. He believed the relationship would compromise the mayor.

I knew Officer Nelthrope was in trouble, and his transfer out the unit was inevitable. In fact, he had transferred out of the EPU to the 7th Precinct by February 2003.

"How do you know that the person at the other end
of the hotline is not part of the conspiracy?"
*Anonymous*

On April 26, 2003 in the morning hours, I received a call from Officer Nelthrope. He started by asking what I was doing. I told him I had just finished feeding my children and putting them down for their nap. He asked if I were sitting down. I replied, "Yes, why?"

He told me that he was in possession of a black notebook and that some high-ranking officials from the Detroit Police Department were en route to his home. I asked who and what was the nature of their business. Nelthrope said he could not give me with the official's name. He did inform me that the notebook contained information about illegal activities of Officers Jackson and Lewis, and Mayor Kilpatrick.

Initially my stomach dropped, and I became speechless. "I'm not sure what you're going to do," I finally responded, "but remember that Mayor Kilpatrick is very vindictive. Do whatever you have to do and have no regrets."

After our conversation, my mind began to run various scenarios of what was about to happen. The house was quiet; the kids were napping; my wife was at work; but I couldn't help thinking that any moment a swarm of black cars would swoop in on Nelthrope. Since I was his crew leader, anything he said or informed was something that I have more than likely witnessed. I thought that within the next hour, the same black cars and men in black suits would be on their way to my house.

"Am I ready for this? What will I say? What will I do?" I visualized Nelthrope being bombarded with questions of who, what, when, where, and how. Worse yet, I could see Nelthrope being physically beaten by both Lewis and Jackson.

For an instant, while my stomach was still rolling and flip-flopping, I wondered if I should anticipate an altercation with Lewis and Jackson. I looked out the window; next, I went to the front and back door to be sure they were locked. I had to clear my head, settle my stomach, and get back to the business of the day. I took a deep breath, counted to 10, and planned my next move.

I felt that it was the right time to make my move. As the hours passed since Nelthrope's call, I had a chance to calm down. I was actually relieved and happy that he had the courage not only to keep a notebook but also to turn it over to Internal Affairs (IA).

I didn't want to be a part of that corrupted administration any longer. The thought of facing Lewis and Jackson now knowing the truth was out made me more apprehensive about what they would do to me. They both had criminal backgrounds and were prone to violence. Anything could set them off and send them in my direction. I felt that I had to leave this administration; the sooner, the better! I felt that I would rather face the uncertainties of the streets than face Kilpatrick, Lewis, and Jackson.

Later on the same day, Nelthrope called and expressed how concerned he was for his safety. He said he had contacted a high-ranking official from the Detroit Police Internal Affairs Unit. However, before they arrived at his home, he received a call from Lewis, who asked him if he had filed a complaint with IA on him and Jackson. Nelthrope's response was negative. Lewis remarked, "I thought we were friends." When Nelthrope finished the call, he immediately donned his bulletproof vest. I asked the question, "If IA is supposed to be confidential, who alerted Officer Lewis?"

❧    ❧

Subsequently, I chose to go back to the precinct. I became a police officer, knowing that patrolling the streets was the backbone of the job, and I had no problem going back to that position. Nelthrope was already at the 7<sup>th</sup> Precinct and other former crew members were there, as well. It was relatively close to home, and I wouldn't have to travel far to work. I could keep a watchful eye on my home while out on "code," which was the department's term for a lunch break. Within the next week, I voluntarily transferred to the 7<sup>th</sup> Precinct.

> "We must not allow ourselves to become like the system we oppose."
> *Bishop Desmond Tutu*

Officers Nelthrope, Tucker, and Conner were all transferred out of the EPU involuntarily by Jackson and Lewis. All three officers went to the 7<sup>th</sup> Precinct on the east side of Detroit. I wanted to leave the EPU; however, Jackson and Kilpatrick twice persuaded me to stay. Kilpatrick said that he really needed me in the unit. Jackson told me he needed me to stay, because I was the mayor's best guy.

I think they wanted me to stay with the unit, because I had witnessed too much corruption and immoral activity. I thought about how I would be received at the precinct by officers and supervisors. Security for the mayor had always been an elite unit, and one didn't voluntarily transfer out.

I knew that Mayor Kilpatrick was very vindictive; he held the city in his hands. I felt that I needed to rise above the fear of potential retaliation and vindictiveness. I made my decision to transfer out the unit, because I didn't want to become corrupt like them!

"Courage is the art of being the only one
who knows you're scared to death."
*Harold Wilson, Baron of Revaulx*

On April 30, 2003, the mayor went out of town and was gone for approximately four days. I chose this time to make my move, despite being afraid. Leaving the EPU was the only way to keep my integrity intact, even though I knew there would be repercussions. However, I had taken an oath, a sworn commitment to act in an ethical manner. I also believed in four key principles. The *badge* that I proudly wore was the symbol of my office. *Integrity* represents my honesty and how I live my life. *Character* is the moral strength and reputation that distinguishes me as an individual. *Courage* is having the fortitude to confront fear and danger and to withstand unethical pressure. I made the decision that I was not going to compromise any one of the four. So, early in the morning at home, I pulled out a DPD transfer form and began typing. I completed a request for a voluntary transfer.

Once the transfer request was completed, however, I faced one problem: the request required the signature of a supervisor. I drove to the mayor's office. I entered the Coleman A. Young Municipal Building and took the rear elevator to the 11th Floor. I entered the mayor's office through the rear door. Just as I made my way to the security office, I ran into Sgt. Malcolm Jordan. I asked him if I could speak with him in private. We stepped into the security office and walked toward the rear. I explained to him that I wanted to voluntarily transfer out the unit.

"I am planning to leave myself," Jordan said. "I'm just waiting on a phone call."

I told Jordan I needed a supervisor's signature in order to proceed with my transfer.

"Give it to me," he said boldly. "I'll sign it. I'm not afraid of any of them." He then signed the transfer. "Good luck, man!"

I thanked him for signing the transfer and immediately felt free. I left the mayor's office and drove to Detroit Police Headquarters, 1300 Beaubien. I presented my police identification to security, quickly jumped on the elevator, and got off at the Chief of Police floor. I took a short walk to the chief's office and rang the buzzer. I identified myself through the intercom system, and the door opened. I spoke with Commander Sharon Mann, presented my voluntary transfer, and asked that it be effective immediately. "Are you sure you want to go to the 7th Precinct?" she asked.

"Yes, ma'am, I am ready to serve the citizens of the community. I'm ready to take police runs."

"Does Al know about this?" she asked.

"No, but I have a sergeant's endorsement."

Commander Mann paused for a moment and then said , "Good luck," as she reluctantly gave her okay. She signed the transfer, and I quickly thanked her for her time.

I exited the chief's office feeling like the weight of the world had been lifted off my shoulders. Before I could reach my vehicle parked in a private lot, Jackson called on my cell. When I answered he said, "I heard you transferred out the unit."

"Yes, I did," I boldly replied.

"Don't you know you have to go through me?" he said angrily.

"No, I don't! I have a sergeant's signature." I turned off the phone. Damn, that felt good! I drove to Max's Bar and had a strong drink with my good friend.

On May 1, 2003, Jackson called my cell and requested that I turn in all my EPU-issued equipment. By this time, I had already boxed up My Glock 27 back-up weapon, ear pieces, lapel pin, SkyPager®, and keys to the mayor's office. I drove to the mayor's office to surrender my equipment. I met Jackson in the security office and handed him the box of equipment. He had a phony smile on his face. "Hey, man, if you need anything, let me know."

I replied, "Thanks and take care."

He then moved in close and gave me the brotherly love hug. I quickly looked over my shoulder expecting someone to stab me in the back or shoot me.

I drove to the 7th Precinct, wondering if the chief's office was going to honor my precinct request. When I arrived at the precinct on Mack and Gratiot, I met with Officer Nelthrope, who was in full uniform and working the front desk. I told him I had just turned in all my equipment. He asked "What date are you to report here?"

"Officer Jackson did not advise on a date," I replied.

Nelthrope told me to hold on and walked to the back office. When he returned, he said, "Man, you report tomorrow on midnights."

I recall saying, "Damn! Al didn't even tell me!" I would have been AWOL (absent without leave) if I had not shown up. I was pleased that my transfer went through and that I received the midnight shift.

Nelthrope showed me around the precinct and introduced me to Inspector Maxwell.

My first midnight shift at the 7th Precinct was on May 2, 2003. I reported for duty at 11:20 p.m. in full uniform. I proceeded downstairs to roll call. When I walked into the room and saw Officer Conner, we spoke briefly. I grabbed an empty chair and waited for the supervisor, Sgt. Steward, to conduct roll call. More officers began to arrive.

I was surprised to see Officer John Bennett arrive. I did not know he was at the 7th Precinct. Officer Bennett was the creator and author of FireJerryO.com (now known as Detroituncovered.com). I had been regularly following his postings and information on his website.

I then observed a bald man with a dark complexion walk into the roll call room. This guy was built like Arnold Schwarzenegger but was African American. After roll call, he walked over to me and said, "You don't remember me, do you?"

As I studied his face he did look familiar, however I could not recall having ever met him. He introduced himself as Marcus Hamilton. "I was the DJ at the party you attended with Mayor Kilpatrick."

"I remember you now. You jammed that party with your music."

# Chapter 10

# Whistleblowers Exposed

Officer Nelthrope contacted Deputy Chief Gary Brown about the corruption that occurred within the Kilpatrick Administration. Brown went to Nelthrope's house for a face-to-face interview and to do more fact collecting about the events he reported. When he began to investigate Mayor Kilpatrick and the wild Manoogian party, he was subsequently terminated from the police department.

Brown had been the deputy chief over the IA (Internal Affairs) Unit and did not hesitate to investigate Nelthrope's complaint. Even though this complaint was about the mayor of Detroit, Brown did not waver in his decision to move forward with the investigation. He followed the proper protocols for handling complaints presented to his department. He did not compromise his integrity by pushing the complaint aside, once he realized the magnitude and depth of the potential investigation. He performed his job with due diligence and truthfulness until his termination.

On May 14, 2003, I was at home watching the news, seeing all the reporters at Nelthrope's residence. A barrage of reporters was on the sidewalk in front of his home interviewing him. The reporters were holding up a confidential IA memo with Nelthrope's name on it. He looked like a deer in the headlights, denying everything the reporters asked him. He could not camouflage the look of terror on his face. He had trusted the system, and the system failed him. In law enforcement, the IA Unit holds the most confidentiality of any other unit. Once the confidential memo on Nelthrope's complaint was shared with the Kilpatrick Administration, it was strategically placed in the hands of the media. Nelthrope was compromised and egregiously exposed, for the sole purpose of intimidation.

"Never believe anything until it has been officially denied."
*Claud Cockburn*

Mayor Kilpatrick stood on the front porch of the Manoogian Mansion and delivered a press conference. He denied all allegations and dismissed the party as a rumor; he claimed he did not have lewd parties. "I don't whore around on my wife. I want people to understand that I would never disrespect my God, my wife, or my children."

I remember watching the news, listening to those words, "I would never disrespect my God," and thinking he made a big mistake. He must have been desperate to bring "God" to his defense. I wondered about a large lightning bolt striking him on the porch. Would people have believed Nelthrope then? I thought why would he invoke the name of God to cover up his misdeeds? I was momentarily shocked. Why was he lying like this?

But then again, around this time I started to believe that Kilpatrick was above the law. He could stand in front of cameras and tell a straight-faced lie, knowing that he had the support of people around him to cover up his lies and misdeeds. I also believed that Kilpatrick felt the walls were closing in on him, and he became desperate to clear his name. When he vehemently denied Nelthrope's allegations, I knew that the City of Detroit was gearing up for a long fight to learn the truth. I'm sure at this moment Kilpatrick had aligned his team of defense and was preparing the troops for war.

> "There are two primary choices in life;
> to accept conditions as they exist,
> or accept the responsibility for changing them."
> *Denis Waitley*

Shortly after transferring to the 7th Precinct, I received subpoenas from the attorney general's office in Lansing and from the Michigan State Police while I was on duty. I quickly learned that Officers Nelthrope, Conner, and Tucker had received subpoenas too. In fact, I later learned that the entire EPU had been subpoenaed. I recall speaking with Officer Tucker in the 7th Precinct lobby; she was very frightened. She was raising two children as a single parent and needed her job. What I gathered from that conversation was that she wasn't going to talk about what she had witnessed. I explained to her that I refuse to lie for the mayor or for Jackson or Lewis.

The day I was assigned to be interviewed by the attorney general and state police came very quickly. I was off duty during the interview, because I had worked the midnight shift. I recall that it was a warm and sunny day around 10 a.m. I entered the building specified on the subpoena and observed another officer leaving. When I entered the interview room, there were three men and a woman. All of the interviewers had notepads and pens. On the table was a tape recorder with a small upright microphone.

The main interviewer introduced himself and the other three, as well as their agencies. As I began to answer questions about Mayor Kilpatrick's relationship with various women, the main interviewer halted me. He stopped the tape recorder and stated that my remarks would be off the record. He turned to the woman from the attorney general's office and proceeded to whisper loudly. "I'm not going to include the mayor's personal life in this investigation. I'll stick to the criminal acts that were carried out or witnessed." He then turned the tape recorder on and said we were back on the record.

I was asked many questions about the Manoogian Mansion party, Officers Lewis and Jackson. I was also asked a number of questions by the woman from the attorney general's office. I knew this was my opportunity to correct the wrongs, not only in the EPU, but also within the Detroit Police Department. I answered all the interviewer's questions and dared not stretch the truth.

When I left the interview, I felt very confident that justice would be served. That confident feeling was later proven to be wrong. Within weeks, the Attorney General Mike Cox declared all allegations unfounded, except for overtime abuse and unreported accidents. He even went so far as to declare the Manoogian party an "urban legend."

Detroit Police Chief Jerry Oliver was absent from justice, by failing to investigate and discipline Jackson and Lewis. This was a slap in the face to the officers who told the truth. So what kind of message did this send to honest cops? Truth and justice meant nothing to the investigation. I continued to honor my badge throughout this travesty. I trusted the system and expected to be treated sincerely and perhaps even lauded for my effort.

> "Whistleblowers can be considered a part of a warning system
> for society to fix problems before they become worse."
> *Brian Martin*

One morning I received a knock at the front door of my eastside home in Detroit. I immediately looked out the upstairs bedroom window and observed two white men standing at the door. I removed my handgun from the holster. I deactivated my house alarm and walked carefully downstairs and eased to the front door. With my gun in hand, I shouted angrily, "Who is it?"

One of them answered, "M. L. Elrick and Ben Schmitt from the Detroit Free Press," as they held up their identification.

I quickly slipped back into the kitchen nook and called Officer Nelthrope. I explained the circumstances, and he advised me to speak with the reporters. He also informed me that they had just left his residence. I quickly asked Nelthrope for a description of the two reporters. I then placed my weapon back in its holster and opened the front door.

The sun was shining brightly. I asked the reporters how I could help them. M. L. Elrick asked if they could come inside and speak with me about Officer Nelthrope. I invited the reporters inside, and they sat on the couch. It was warm downstairs, so I opened the French doors in the living room where we were sitting. I sat in a chair directly opposite the reporters.

M. L. Elrick led the questioning by asking if I had seen the news and all the media that was camped out at Nelthrope's home. I responded by saying I was shocked about the ambush and the leaked confidential memo. I told both reporters that what they witnessed was the power of Mayor Kilpatrick.

"The time is always right to do what is right."
*Dr. Martin Luther King, Jr.*

"What could you tell me about Officers Jackson and Lewis and the EPU?" Elrick asked.

I paused for a moment and looked down at the hardwood floor. I was thinking whether I should do the right thing or the safe thing. I looked up at the reporters and said, "Do you really want to know? And are you sure you want to know?"

They looked at me intensely and said, "Yes" with their pens and notebooks in the ready position.

I paused again and thought about my fellow officers in the EPU, the newly fired Gary Brown, and my friend Harold Nelthrope. I made up my mind to tell the truth in hopes that the reporters would get the information out and that something would be done to correct the wrongs of Jackson and Lewis. I had no idea that exposing them would bring repercussions on me and on my family as a consequence of what was to happen next to me.

There was a price to pay for telling the truth and exposing Jackson and Lewis. However, I never dreamed that as a police officer, by exposing the truth, I was putting my career and life on the line. Whatever happened to truth and justice?

I explained to the reporters why I left the unit and about its high turnover rate. I talked about overtime fraud, unreported vehicle accidents, and drinking on the job by Jackson and Lewis. I shared my concern about Kilpatrick's safety. He was blinded by his friendship with Jackson and Lewis.

During this interview, I never shared any of the immoral acts of the mayor with other women. I talked only about the wrongdoings of Jackson and Lewis. Both reporters thanked me for the information and said the article would appear in the Detroit News and Free Press on Saturday, May 24, 2003. I shook their hands and escorted them to the front door. After they left, I called Nelthrope and informed him that I had his back.

> "The ultimate measure of a man is not
> where he stands in moments of comfort and convenience,
> but where he stands at times of challenge and controversy."
> *Dr. Martin Luther King, Jr.*

On May 24, 2003, as I entered the 7th Precinct at approximately 7:20 a.m., 40 minutes from the end of my tour of duty, fellow officers approached me. "Way to go, Walt! Have you read today's paper? You're one brave man."

I picked up the local newspaper from the front counter and read the article written by M. L. Elrick and Ben Schmitt entitled "Pal Runs Security like Tyrant, Cop Says."

# Pal runs security like tyrant, cops say

BY M.L. ELRICK, JIM SCHAEFER
AND BEN SCHMITT
FREE PRESS STAFF WRITERS

➤ Editorial: No excuses. 12A.

I started reading the article, pausing now and then to look around the large lobby to see who was watching my reactions. I tried to remain expressionless. I would have preferred to read the article at home, since it was so close to the end of my shift. I just couldn't wait; I stood there in uniform and held the newspaper tightly with both hands. I was eager to read what the reporters had written after my face-to-face interview. I was concerned that they had put a twist on the story or embellished the information I shared.

After reading the article, however, I was relieved that their journalism was based on good integrity. I felt that both reporters could be considered trustworthy. Afterward, I knew without a doubt that this was going to force Chief Jerry Oliver to step in and deliver justice. I felt that he would go to the mayor's office and pull Jackson and Lewis from the unit and reprimand them for their actions.

While still in the lobby, I thumbed through the rest of the newspaper. Another article caught my attention. It exposed the background information on Kevin Lewis. Up to this point I had no prior knowledge of his questionable past. The headline was titled "Mayoral Cop, Drug Kingpin Are Linked."

The story described Kevin Lewis's friendship with the brother of a notorious drug dealer. Lewis was never charged in connection to any of the drug dealer's activities, but the brother, Peter McGuire, was later convicted for running drugs from Detroit to South Carolina. The article also covered another incident associated with the drug dealer's brother involving Lewis outside a café in downtown Detroit. Allegedly drunk, he fired up to 11 shots from a .40 caliber Glock handgun toward a group of men and grazed the wrist of one of them. Witnesses reported that Lewis was yelling, "I'm going to kill your boy," according to court records. It was reported that he was acting in self-defense after someone attacked his passenger, Peter McGuire. Lewis was charged with "assault with intent to murder and felonious use of a firearm." However, he was subsequently convicted of a misdemeanor gun charge.

When I read that, I had a better understanding of who Lewis really was. I also connected the gun charge incident to the story he told me in DC. He said he had needed to hire a high-priced attorney to get him out of trouble.

After I read both articles, I had a sickening feeling that consequences and repercussions would ensue from Lewis and possibly his buddy Jackson. As I drove home that morning I realized that I could be in danger. I envisioned various scenarios of Lewis with his drug friends trying to ambush me as I got out of my car. I now possessed true fear for myself and my family!

I immediately began to question myself non-stop. What have I gotten myself into? Should I have told the reporters nothing? If I knew of Lewis's background, would I have taken the risks?

I pulled into my driveway and resolved that it was time to see this through and uphold the truth, regardless of what followed. I had to put my trust in God that He would protect and sustain my family, should anything happen to me.

> "Being right will not feed your family or pay the mortgage."
> *Anonymous*

I reported for duty at the 7th Precinct on July 8, 2003 and was downstairs standing by for roll call. I was astounded to see Chief Jerry Oliver walk into the roll call room. It wasn't commonplace for him to attend roll call, and a midnight shift roll call, at that!

I smiled at him.

"How are you, Walter?" he asked.

I replied, "Just fine, Chief Oliver. Thanks."

Chief Oliver and his driver took a seat along the wall. I wondered if the chief was there to ask me about Lewis and Jackson. I started to get excited and hoped that he would uphold my support of Officer Nelthrope.

I could hardly focus on Sgt. Steward's words at roll call, as my mind was occupied with why the chief was there. Because he was in the building, all of the brass came down to roll call. Again this wasn't the usual attendance for a typical shift. Lieutenant Barney Frazier entered the room, and every officer stood up and fell into formation. At the end of roll call, Chief Oliver requested to speak with Officer Bennett. I was completely disappointed.

The buzz in the precinct was that the chief had sent Officer Bennett home. We later learned that the chief admonished him about his website, FireJerryO.com. He was suspended with pay, pending removal of the site by morning. Chief Oliver explained that the site contained racial slurs which were detrimental to the department. He concluded that if the site was still up in the morning, Bennett would be suspended without pay. Bennett continued to operate the site while on suspension. I believed that he was a genuine truth fighter!

Chief Oliver never approached me to inquire about the newspaper article and the actions I reported about Jackson and Lewis. I began to believe that he must have been in support of these men, as well as Mayor Kilpatrick.

I continued my duty responsibilities to the community of the 7th Precinct. It was a busy shift and a busy precinct. Officer Marcus Hamilton became my regular partner. When he decided to work with me as a regular assignment, I gave him specific details about the illegal and immoral activity I witnessed at the mayor's office. I expressed how Kilpatrick was very vindictive and at some point might try to ruin my career. My partner listened, and he still requested to be assigned as my regular partner. He was a dedicated officer, and we worked well together. We even became close friends and attended the same church.

# Chapter 11

# Retaliation Begins

"If you speak the truth, have a foot in the stirrup."
*Turkish proverb*

The summer moved on, and I found working the streets again exhilarating. A dedicated officer who worked hard, I was awarded two Detroit Police Department certificates of commendation. The first was the result of my actions on June 1, 2003. Officer Conner and I responded to a police run about an armed citizen. The perpetrator was accosting and robbing women while they either entered or exited their vehicles. After completing an initial report and investigation, I located and arrested the perpetrator at Detroit Receiving Hospital. By arresting this perpetrator, the Detroit Police Department was able to close the case on eight other felony cases.

The second commendation was for my actions on June 10, 2003. While Officer Hamilton and I were on patrol, we initiated a traffic stop for littering. Upon investigating the driver and the vehicle, I observed the ignition was punched. The vehicle was reported stolen, and the driver and four passengers were arrested for possession of a stolen motor vehicle. The driver was also wanted for armed robbery. I was serving the community and making a difference; that was all I wanted to do.

Unfortunately, I felt the commendations were overshadowed by bogus citizens' complaints that began soon after I left the EPU. The first of four complaints occurred as a result of events on May 8, 2003.

I was assigned a female partner, Officer Jane Collins. We were dispatched to a police run in the area of Edwin and Olympia. Upon our arrival there, I observed three units already on the scene. When my partner exited the car, she immediately fell into a manhole and injured her leg. The injury occurred because it was after midnight and the manhole cover was missing. We never made contact with the complainants or any suspects.

I immediately transported my partner to the emergency room of Detroit Receiving Hospital. After she was treated and released, we returned to the precinct. She completed the proper documents about her injury, and I was assigned to work the desk. Her injury left me with no partner for the remaining time of my shift. It was not until July 25, 2003 that Lt. Frazier notified me of a citizen's complaint.

Apparently a citizen had called in a complaint at 2:30 a.m. on May 8, 2003. A 45-year-old man stated that an officer used excessive force, and that he was flung onto a scout car, slapped in the face, and hit in the eye. He described the offending officer as a Black man in his late thirties, 5'9", 200 pounds, with a bald head and dark complexion. He described the second officer on the scene as a Black man in his late thirties, 5'7", 250 pounds, medium complexion.

I was issued written orders to a Garrity interview at Internal Affairs. After reading the citizen's complaint report, I tried to explain to Lt. Frazier that neither my partner nor I met the descriptions. I also told him that on that night, I had a female partner who was hurt as we arrived at the scene; thus we never stayed long enough to make contact with any suspects. I told him that our squad car video recording would show that we had nothing to do with this complaint.

To my dismay, Lt. Frazier didn't want to hear my side of the story. He walked away without responding to my explanations.

A Garrity interview goes by several different names, including the Garrity Right, Law or Warning. By invoking the Garrity Rule, the officer is invoking his or her right against self-incrimination. Any statements given will be used for department investigations and not for criminal prosecution purposes.

On July 29, 2003, I reported to Internal Affairs. I told them what had happened that night and how my female partner was injured, forcing us to leave the scene. After the IA interview, no action was taken, and I was released from this complaint. Sadly more complaints were to follow.

The second complaint occurred as the result of a traffic stop initiated the morning of June 9, 2003, just prior to the end of our midnight shift. Officer Hamilton was the driver, and I was the scout unit passenger, also known as the jump man. We observed a vehicle travel into an intersection and come to a screeching halt. The driver had disregarded a red light, traveling beyond the signal light. After skidding to a stop, the driver remained in the middle of the intersection. We looked at each other as if to say, "Did you see that? Is this person trying to get our attention?"

Officer Hamilton put on the scout car lights to signal the driver to pull over. The driver was a white female who was belligerent toward my partner from the first contact. I observed from the opposite side of the car. As the jump man, I did not make any contact with the driver. However, it was my job to document the stop and write the traffic ticket, while Hamilton interacted with the driver and monitored the scene.

The driver had trouble producing her vehicle registration. She was issued two citations, one for disregarding the red light and the other for not having valid registration. I was informed on July 11, 2003 by Sgt. Ken Russo, the 7th Precinct supervisor, that the driver had lodged a complaint against me.

The driver complained that the traffic stop lasted 45 minutes. In her complaint, she wrote that her uncle, a retired Detroit police lieutenant, advised her that a stop of this length was essentially an arrest. She also objected to receiving two traffic tickets.

I was summoned to IA for a Garrity interview. Sgt. Steward reviewed the in-car videotape and discovered that the traffic stop took only 17 minutes, of which eight minutes were spent waiting for her to produce her driver's license and registration. The videotape exonerated me from the citizen's complaint.

Afterward, Sgt. Steward waved me into a private room and told me to be careful, because "they are watching you." I felt that this was his way of warning me that more complaints or possible retaliation was yet to come.

During this time in my career with the Detroit Police Department, I made it a point to document all of my work. I believed that it was more important to do so now more than ever. I also believed that whoever was behind the complaints were targeting me. If "they" are watching me, who are they? I had to believe that it was a combination of Jackson and Lewis, along with Kilpatrick and Oliver. I think that they wanted to discredit me and tarnish my service record. The next complaint gave me reason to believe that I should consider taking a stress leave before a more serious complaint was lodged against me.

The third complaint was certainly bogus! It was a citizen's complaint in which the description of the offending officer could not possibly have been me. I think the purpose was to pad my file with citizens' complaints. Even if they are proven to been unfounded, the complaints could still tarnish my reputation. It could possibly put me on IA's radar, and subsequent complaints might be harder to disprove.

I was given a copy of the IA request for a Garrity interview from Sgt. Russo on August 21, 2003. I was also handed a copy of the citizen's complaint. The complaint was given by a 28-year-old female reporting improper conduct of an officer. Her complaint stemmed from an altercation she had with a male suspect. She complained that I witnessed a man hit her in the face and did nothing about it. She called for police help, because the man was accosting her in the parking lot of a local bar. He allegedly harassed her and took her money. She also complained that my partner, Officer Hamilton, and I left the scene where the male suspect subsequently forced her into his car, took her to an unknown location, and raped her. She complained that we did not help her.

The complainant described me as a white male or one with a very light complexion, medium build, bald head, and 5'5". She described my partner as a white male with no other descriptors. I explained to Sgt. Russo that I did not fit the description of either officer. "Look at me. I'm 6'4", 290 pounds, and my partner is at least 6'1, 225 pounds, and neither of us is light or white. Hamilton has a darker complexion, and I am not one you would consider 'very light.'"

I looked Sgt. Russo in the eyes. "If I get one more bogus citizen's complaint, I am going off-duty on a stress leave." I was shocked that so many complaints were coming in from routine police runs such as this one.

On August 2, 2003, at 5:35 a.m., Officer Hamilton and I were dispatched to Concord and Mack Avenue about an assault. Upon our arrival, only one vehicle was in the parking lot. I spoke with the driver behind the wheel of that vehicle. He was a security officer for the establishment and was responsible for the parking lot. He had no knowledge of an assault or any situation with a male and female. I looked in the restaurant and observed no customers. I drove around the immediate area and failed to locate a complainant. I never had any interaction with a female at this location.

I had documented all of the information about this police run on my run sheet. It summarized that I responded to the assault called in by dispatch. There was no female or male at the scene to speak to about an assault. Upon investigating the scene and speaking to the security officer, my partner and I left the area. The run sheet was given to the duty supervisor at the end of my tour of duty.

I told all of this to the IA investigators during my Garrity interview. It should be noted that each time I searched the file cabinet for the original run sheet, it was not there; I believe that it was removed from the packet. The complaint was later found to be unwarranted against me or my partner. However, the mental stress of going through the Garrity process yet again was beginning to wear me down.

It wasn't until October 3, 2003 that the next citizen's complaint occurred. This one was the last straw. I have never robbed or stolen anything from anyone in my entire life, and I certainly didn't start then. The day started as any other. At 10:45 p.m., I was awakened from a deep sleep by my alarm clock. I sat on the side of the bed thinking how grateful I was to get a good amount of sleep with three small kids in the house.

I took a hot shower and listened to the news at 11 o'clock while I dressed. I thought that the crime in the city was really getting out of hand. I sat on the end of the bed and put on my freshly shined black leather boots. I laced up each boot tightly and positioned my back-up weapon on my ankle. I emptied the handgun and checked the barrel for any obstruction. I then placed it back in the ankle holster. I put on my bullet-proof vest and checked the front of my shirt to make sure my name tag, badge, and awards ribbons were in place.

After putting on my shirt, I reached in the closet for my gun belt and secured it on my waist with the belt keepers. I rocked my gun belt up and down to make sure it remained in place. I then removed my 40 cal. Glock from the holster and the magazine and bullet from the chamber. I checked the weapon and barrel for obstructions before performing 10 quick draws. I reloaded my weapon and placed it back in the holster.

I went into kids' rooms and give them hugs and kisses, while whispering "I love you" to each of them.

I headed downstairs with my briefcase and kissed my wife goodbye. She was always there to see me off to work. At the back door, I made it a habit of peering out the window before going out to make sure no one was laying in wait. I told my wife I loved her and the kids.

I entered my Ford Expedition and turned on the jazz station. I looked around as I pulled out of my driveway, checking the front of my house, as well as the neighbor's. While cruising into work, I thought about what situations I might encounter on duty that night, getting my mind geared up.

I arrived at the precinct and saw my partner in the parking lot in his car. As I approached, he exited his car and said, "What's up, doc?"

"Ain't nothing going on, man," I said.

We entered the precinct together and checked our patrol assignments. We walked downstairs to the roll call and before I could reach the room door, Sgt. Fred Steward called out, "Harris!"

I saw him waving his hand for me to come closer. "Harris, you and your partner have a hot run! Grab your stuff and head out to a shots-fired run."

At that point, I was very suspicious of any and all activity going on in the precinct. I looked around and thought, why us with all these other officers sitting here? I swung my briefcase around and started back upstairs with my partner. I really didn't mind taking the shots-fired call, because I loved gun runs and the adrenaline needed to get the job done.

Upstairs we signed out prep radios and a shotgun. Officer Hamilton grabbed the keys to our car, and we were out the door.

> "Every time I've done something
> that doesn't feel right,
> it ended up not being right."
> *Mario Cuomo*

We walked through the dimly lit parking lot searching for vehicle code #003423. I noticed it was not our regularly assigned vehicle. I turned to my partner and said, "This is not our car. Why would they put us in this car?"

My partner unlocked the car doors and pressed the trunk release button. After placing my briefcase in the trunk, I entered the vehicle and noticed how dirty it was. I then observed that something was missing. "There is no camera in this car," I told him as he settled into the driver's seat. "We can't use it!"

"Let's take this shots-fired run and then come back and switch vehicles," Hamilton suggested. I explained to him that everything must be documented. I refused to go on patrol without a camera.

"Pull the vehicle into the precinct garage," I told him. In the garage, I exited the scout car and entered the precinct. I walked to the front desk. I met Sgt. Steward. "What are you still doing here? I sent you and your partner on a shots-fired run."

"There is no camera in the car, and I refuse to answer a run without a video camera," I said.

Sgt. Steward appeared to be angry. "Y'all need to answer that run right now!" He pointed to the door.

I stood my ground, because the whole scenario just did not feel right. "I'm not going on one police run without a video camera," I repeated boldly.

The exchange between Sgt. Steward and me went on for approximately 15 minutes. Finally he agreed to put a camera in the vehicle. We went into the precinct garage, and he unlocked the video camera storage cabinet. He removed a video camera from the shelf and sat in the front passenger seat. He complained the entire time he was installing the camera. After connecting the proper wires, he placed a blank videocassette into the recorder. He checked to see if the video recorder was working properly and then locked the recorder box. Only the supervisors had access to the videocassettes.

I thanked Sgt. Steward for installing the camera, and my partner and I pulled out of the garage. Each night before Hamilton and I left the parking lot, we bowed our heads, held hands, and prayed for protection, wisdom, and the ability to treat people fairly. That night was no different, even given the "hot run" call. After our prayer, we advised dispatch we were en route to the assigned run.

As we were driving to the fired-shots site, we discussed the timing of the call. Normally, we received calls from dispatch. This call was unusual, because it came directly from the roll call supervisor. Why me? If it was so urgent, other officers were already present in the roll call room. That was the first red flag of the night.

We also discussed why it took the supervisor so long to install the camera. It wasn't installed until 12:05 a.m., and we had been assigned a vehicle that wasn't our standard vehicle. These were the next two red flags.

We pulled out of the parking lot at 12:25 a.m. and arrived at the location of the 5000 block of Parker Street, not far from the intersection of Van Dyke and East Warren Avenue, by 12:30 a.m. As we approached Parker Street, we turned off our headlights and slowed down. I contacted dispatch and advised we were at the scene.

As soon as we arrived, the fourth red flag went up for me. It had been at least 45 minutes by the time we arrived at the location, and the suspect vehicle was still at the scene. Typically when we arrived at a shots-fired location, the suspect vehicle would have already left. On this night a blue Chevy Impala, which matched the description given by Sgt. Steward, was slowly pulling away from the curb, as if it were waiting for our arrival. We turned on our headlights and overhead berries and cherries (red and blue lights). I told my partner to turn on his spotlight.

The vehicle stopped in the middle of the street. We exited our scout car, and my partner approached the driver side of the suspect vehicle. I approached on the passenger side of the vehicle in a cover position. I quickly observed four people in the automobile. There were two men in the front seat and two women in the back seat. I told my partner to make sure everything we did was in front of the video camera.

We shouted very loudly and clearly, "Let me see your hands. Everyone: let me see your hands." We then ordered everyone to place their hands on the front and rear windshield. My partner ordered the driver to turn off the car and throw the keys out the window. Everyone was removed from the vehicle and frisked for weapons by Officer Hamilton. He made contact and searched each person, while I covered him for officer safety.

Once everyone was searched and secured, I searched the automobile for weapons. No weapons were recovered, and there were no bullet holes in the vehicle. I told my partner to make sure he explained to the occupants the nature of the police run. I also told him to explain why we took such action.

After my partner so advised the occupants, he said, "Let's get out of here." I quickly stopped my partner and advised him to get everyone's names, identifiers, and addresses. He made all contact with the occupants of the vehicle, and I documented their information on the run sheet.

During this time, another red flag went up. We had gone on a gun run, and no one backed us. No other squad car arrived on the scene to assist. After collecting the occupant's identifiers, I ran their names through the National Crime Information Center, and none was wanted. The occupants were released at the scene, and we left.

As we were pulling away, I asked my partner "Wasn't that unusual, no one backing us on that run?"

We proceeded with the rest of our tour. We typically checked local businesses, so we started with the Marathon station that was near Gratiot Avenue and Van Dyke. There were no panhandlers or carjackers loitering at that time. We continued checking on other businesses.

We received a police run at 1:35 a.m. to 7800 East Jefferson Avenue in reference to an assault and battery. Upon our arrival, I spoke with a man and woman who were arguing. I counseled the couple on forgiveness, relationships, and responsibilities. No assault occurred during the argument, and they both became civil toward each other prior to our leaving. I advised both subjects of disorderly conduct and left their apartment.

At 2:30 a.m., I received a call from dispatch to report to the 7th Precinct, per Lieutenant Barney Frazier. Dispatch then advised me to go straight to the lieutenant's office. I acknowledged dispatch, and we began driving back to the precinct. En route, I asked my partner, "What is this all about? What does Frazier want with me?"

My partner, who hated Lt. Frazier, said, "I don't know what that coward wants. Maybe he just wants to harass us!"

We pulled into the precinct parking lot and a female officer met us. "Hey, guys, a man called the station and stated y'all robbed him!"

"Girl, you better stop playing with us!"

She stated again (boldly), "Harris, a man just called and stated y'all robbed him. I'm not playing." She walked quickly back into the precinct.

I turned to my partner. "This is what I was explaining to you about the mayor's office. They're trying their best to set me up and ruin me."

"I got your back, man!" my partner said.

We walked into the precinct garage. I looked at my partner and remarked, "I wonder when this bogus robbery was supposed to have taken place."

After entering the precinct through the garage, I walked into the lieutenant's office as directed by dispatch. "Hey, Lt. Frazier, you need to see me?"

He was bent over his desk, with his uniform shirt unbuttoned and tee shirt exposed. He pointed to Fred Steward. "You need to talk to him," and Frazier walked out the room.

I walked over to another desk where Sgt. Steward was sitting. "Hey, Sarge, what's going on?"

Sgt. Steward asked, "Where is your partner?"

I looked over my shoulder and replied, "I thought he was behind me. You want me to go get him?"

He said, "No, don't go anywhere, and don't go into your pockets."

Stunned, I asked, "Don't go into my pockets? What's going on here?"

By this time my partner walked into the office. "Walt, what's going on?"

Sgt. Steward quickly interrupted and asked if we had responded to a police run at the 500 block of Parker Street. I responded, "Yes, that's the shots-fired run you sent us on before roll call".

He instructed my partner and me not to go into our pockets and to surrender the scout car keys. "You need to inform us why you are taking these actions against us!" I demanded.

"A man called into the station and reported that y'all robbed him of $120 and a pair of expensive Cartier glasses. He stated the big one did it, and he thought the same officer robbed him last week too."

I explained to Sgt. Steward that I never had had any contact with the complainant in the past. I never made contact with the complainant earlier that night during the assigned police run. My partner spoke with each person and collected their identifiers, while I covered him during the investigation.

Sgt. Steward advised us to take a seat in the office and that Internal Affairs officers were on their way.

I looked over at my partner and said, "I predicted this day would come, the day that I would get set up."

In the back of my mind I asked myself if Kilpatrick would go that far. Would he do this to ruin my creditability and my career? I leaned in close to my partner and apologized for getting him caught up in Kilpatrick's web.

I turned to Sgt. Steward, who was acting fidgety with paperwork strewn on his desk. He even was starting to sweat. Every time I pressed him about what was going on, he would say, "I ain't in this."

Next, I requested my police union steward, Officer Dunlap. He was promptly dispatched to the lieutenant's office.

While we waited for IA, Sgt. Steward asked to see my police run sheet. I walked over to his desk and surrendered it. He examined it and said out loud, "He said he was in the car by himself! He said he was in the car by himself!" Sgt. Steward looked baffled.

I explained to him that there were four people in the vehicle, in reference to the shots-fired police run. I gave details about the two men in the front seat and two women in the rear seat. I explained how I made sure my partner collected all of their identifiers (social security numbers, dates of birth, race, driver's license numbers, and addresses). Finally, I told Sgt. Steward that if he viewed the videotape from our scout car, all of this could be easily cleared up.

Sgt. Steward threw both his hands up and said, "Hey, Harris, I'm not in this!"

I looked him in his eyes. "I understand you're just doing your job." In the back of my mind I thought, what a coward.

All of the evidence to exonerate me on the spot was present; however, Sgt. Steward continued to carry out what I believed to be Kilpatrick's mission.

Officer Dunlap, an older officer, entered the office dressed in a blue denim jacket and pants. I equated wisdom with his age.

I came quickly to the point about the circumstances.

"At this point, we can request Internal Affairs to present a search warrant," Dunlap said.

I boldly made it clear that I had nothing to hide, and that a search warrant was unnecessary. I told Dunlap that if someone would pull the videotape from my scout car, I would be cleared immediately. He rocked side to side in the swivel chair. "I don't believe they're offering that option," he responded. He knew that IA was going to pull the tape and take it as evidence.

I made sure I expressed to Sgt. Steward that this whole ordeal was very stressful. I also told him that once IA completed their initial investigation that night, I was going to take a stress leave from the Detroit Police Department. I had admonished supervisors earlier that if I received one more bogus citizen complaint, I would do that.

Internal Affairs crew—three men and one woman—arrived at the precinct at 3:05 a.m. dressed in trench coats and brimmed hats, and carrying briefcases. The female officer read our Miranda warning and requested that we surrender our wallets. One male officer conducted a pat-down search of my police uniform. I was in full uniform with a badge on my chest and a gun on my hip. At that moment I felt violated. I felt like a common criminal. It was even more embarrassing, because other officers walked past the glass-enclosed office and witnessed the search.

While Internal Affairs searched me, two precinct officers walked into the room. They were in total shock; their eyes opened wide in amazement; they covered their mouths and quickly left.

IA requested the keys to my scout car and my locker number. After the search of my person, the female officer searched my wallet. "Do you always carry a thousand dollars in your wallet in hundred-dollar bills?" she asked.

"Is it a crime for an officer to carry a thousand dollars?" I responded with my own pointed question.

She responded by stating, "Oh, yeah, it is a pay week."

"That thousand dollars is not part of my paycheck," I corrected her. (I always kept a thousand dollars on hand in the event my family and I had to flee Detroit. I wasn't taking any chances with Kilpatrick and his cronies.)

One of the male officers returned to the office and stated that the scout car was clear. He then handed the female officer a videotape and said, "This needs to be logged in with an evidence tag."

I looked at the tape and wondered if it would disappear. I also wondered if IA was willing to carry out Kilpatrick's mission.

The female officer examined our police run sheet and commented, "He lied; he said he was by himself!" The police run sheet provided evidence that the complainant fabricated his story. IA officers said they would conduct their investigation, after collecting a copy of the police run sheet and videotape. After treating me like a criminal and completely humiliating me, IA left the precinct. Mayor Kilpatrick had succeeded in humiliating me as he and his administration contrived to charge me with larceny. (The charge actually would have been armed robbery, because I had a handgun on my duty belt.)

Still, my major anxiety that night was over the safekeeping of the videotape that IA had confiscated from my scout car. It had captured the entire vehicle stop and investigation. The videotape clearly showed all four occupants in the vehicle and proved I had had no contact with any of them.

> "Don't dwell on what went wrong.
> Instead, focus on what to do next.
> Spend your energies on moving
> forward toward finding the answer."
> *Denis Waitley*

During the early morning hours of October 4, 2003, after I had been falsely accused of armed robbery, I knew my career with the Detroit Police Department was over. It was so satisfying to know that I had listened to that small voice that told me to have a video camera installed in my scout car (I know without a doubt, that it was the Lord speaking to me). I was fed up with the bogus citizens' complaints, along with the lack of support from my supervisors. The armed robbery set-up truly was the last straw!

Given the history of Kilpatrick's connections with the attorney general's office and the chief of police, I knew I couldn't get any help from their offices. I had witnessed the attorney general closing the Michigan State Police investigation of Kilpatrick and announcing that the allegations of the Manoogian party were "urban legends." This gave me the impression that it is not what you know but what you can prove, and that Kilpatrick was untouchable. Thus, going to the state police or the FBI would not have helped me in my situation. There was no agency that would rush in and stop the harassment, rally to my defense, or save my job. In the end, I knew that my livelihood and safety were in peril. The harassment and fear for my safety and well-being caused me to immediately take a duty-related stress leave of absence. I felt like the whole administration was stepping on me as if I were an ant. I knew my law enforcement career was dead.

As I reflected on the summer since leaving the EPU, I realized that the citizens' complaints were ruses to make me look like a rogue cop and to discredit my reputation. It was public knowledge that I was friends with Officer Nelthrope and would possibly be called to testify in a civil case on his behalf. I witnessed corruption in the mayor's office and exposed those acts to the offices of the attorney general, Michigan State Police, and the chief of the Detroit Police Department. I also spoke with reporters from the local newspaper detailing some of the illegal and immoral acts committed by the mayor and his administration. I strongly believed that the mayor's administration, along with Detroit Police Department, mounted a campaign to destroy me. I firmly believe that Sgt. Steward was part of the larceny set-up, because of his direct participation and actions that night. That last citizen's complaint was planned as a robbery set-up. The mayor and his supporters wanted me fired from the police department and in jail, by any means necessary. This was their nefarious way of discrediting and censoring me.

# Chapter 12

# Harassment, Intimidation & Threats

The new wave of harassment came with the demand that I prove why I needed a duty-related stress leave. The Detroit Police Medical Section wanted me to take a family medical leave and use my own sick time. There was no illness that would support a family medical leave; I was under undue stress from my job. This was the administration's way of breaking me financially, forcing me to use my stored and earned sick time. This tactic was often used on whistleblowers. If I had agreed to use my own sick time and exhaust it, I would have ended up being taken off the payroll. I would have had no income, no job.

Lieutenant Frazier ordered me to report to the Psychiatry Crisis Walk-in Clinic on October 6, 2003. When I arrived there, I spoke with Dr. Handly who said I would work on restricted duty until Dr. Jacob Rainey saw me.

The next day, a 7th Precinct supervisor ordered me to report to the Detroit Police Department Medical Section. I arrived at 7:30 a.m. and spoke with Sergeant Catherine Schmidt. She told me that I had been placed on restricted duty (inside work only) and not in uniform. She also informed me that I had an appointment with Dr. Rainey on October 10, 2003 at the Psychiatry Crisis Center.

"Arrogance and rudeness are training wheels on the bicycle of life
for weak people who cannot keep their balance without them."
*Laura Teresa Marquez*

I reported to the Psychiatry Crisis Center for my appointment with Dr. Rainey. I believe that one of the first lines of defense against a whistleblower is to send him or her to be examined by a psychiatrist. The powers that be will mount a campaign to make the whistleblower just imagine the wrongdoing that he or she reported. The whistleblower is then labeled mentally ill and loses his or her credibility.

I wasn't going back to work for fear of retaliation by those that supported Kilpatrick. Was this anxiety? Maybe, but this ordeal was real and ever-evolving. I have never stolen anything in my life. Robbing a civilian while armed and in uniform is completely out of character for me. Many people that I have encountered in my life could affirm that robbery is something I would never do. So, did the department think I was capable of this? Maybe, but going to see a psychiatrist seemed more likely that the department wanted to discredit me and make me out to be crazy. As if I had imagined the complaints and the IA patting me down and emptying my pockets like a common criminal.

Dr. Rainey met me in the lobby and escorted me to a private room and closed the door. I sat down and observed him. He was dressed in a white shirt, tie, and slacks. His hair was neatly trimmed, but he appeared to be arrogant, like one of my college professors.

He pulled out a pad and pencil and asked, "What's going on?"

I explained to him that I voluntarily had transferred out of the EPU, was subpoenaed by the attorney general's office, and told the truth about corruption in the mayor's office. I also shared with him how I had spoken to local newspaper reporters, and finally about what I witnessed Jackson and Lewis had done in the unit. I told him about the bogus citizen complaints and the recent accusation of robbery. At first, I was relieved to get all of these events off my chest. That was until I heard Dr. Rainey's response.

First, he asked me why I talked to reporters and spoke out against what happened during the state police investigation. I explained to him that I had told the truth, which a police officer should do.

Dr. Rainey's next remarks sent shivers down my spine. It proved that he was part of the enemy camp! "You talked to the newspapers. You were the squeaky wheel; now you have to suffer the consequences."

"By not reporting illegal activity, police officers themselves are participants in organized crime," I said.

I believe Dr. Rainey felt no guilt about calling me the squeaky wheel! However, he did ask if I had friends in any other precinct or unit. I paused, because I knew he was a part of the adversary's camp

*Badge of Honor: Blowing the Whistle*

and may have wanted me to expose anyone who could potentially help me. I responded by answering "No, regardless of where I go, the mayor still has control over the police department."

Dr. Rainey gave me the impression that he was an instrument of the police department to do their dirty work. He was not there to assess if I needed medical attention. In fact, he tried to agitate me more to see if I would become aggressive or violent.

I remained calm and stated the facts as I knew them to be. I gave him simple, straightforward answers to his barrage of questions. Little did he know that because of his arrogance and the sense that he was not unbiased, it was infuriating me! I had to maintain my composure while suppressing thoughts of jumping across the table and snatching him up by his collar. I wanted to scream in his face, "Do the right thing! Stop being a pansy, carrying out an evil act for a dollar!"

Of course, I never did that, but for one moment it would have felt good to at least yell back at him. I'm glad I didn't. It probably would have given him reason to commit me!

Dr. Rainey repeatedly stated that I needed to go back to work, but I continually answered no in a reserved manner, stating I could not return to work anymore. Finally I left the Psychiatry Crisis Center and drove to the Detroit Police Medical Section.

Upon my arrival there at 9:30 a.m., I talked to Sgt. Schmidt. She informed me that Dr. Rainey assigned me to off-duty status using my own sick time. She also made me aware that I must seek a psychiatrist on my own. I cautioned Sgt. Schmidt that it was wrong to force me to use my own sick time. I explained how this whole tribulation derived from work on duty.

I was surprised by her next comment. "I am not part of this." It left me with the feeling that she knew something was going on behind the scenes. Was her "this" part of the retaliation I felt was happening on behalf of Mayor Kilpatrick?

She next informed me that I had to return to the medical section in two weeks. Before I left, she handed me a packet containing information on how to apply for the family leave act.

While driving home, I contacted Officer Nelthrope on my cell. I explained to him the circumstances of my appointments with Dr. Rainey and Sgt. Schmidt. He told me he would contact his psychiatrist, Dr. Joseph Neumann, and make him aware of the situation.

By the time I arrived home, Nelthrope advised me that Dr. Neumann's office was expecting my call. I set up an appointment for later the same day.

I arrived at Dr. Neumann's office and checked in with the receptionist. I wondered what the visit would be like. People were entering and leaving the office. I sat straight in my chair to keep people from thinking I was there because I was crazy. I looked around the office as if to say, "I'm okay. What's wrong with you?"

The door opened and a soft-spoken man called my name. I followed Dr. Neumann to his office and immediately began to examine my surroundings. I notice the art work and all the golf paraphernalia in his office. I sat across from him at his desk. I felt compelled to try to read his body language and demeanor. My first impression was that he was laid-back, calm, and patient.

As Dr. Neumann and I began to dialogue, he jotted some notes on a small index card. After explaining everything in detail (bogus citizen complaints, robbery set-up, Internal Affairs investigation, and comments made by supervisors), I felt that he listened. I believed that he understood my concerns. This was in contrast to the police department's doctor who wouldn't listen to me and seemed very adversarial. The first doctor gave me the impression that he was out for the department's best interest, not mine. I didn't feel like a patient talking to a concerned healthcare provider. I felt more like a criminal who was being interrogated and berated by a "bad cop".

Sitting in Dr. Neumann's office, however, I quickly realized that he was a concerned healthcare professional. As our time together went on, I relaxed my guarded posture and communicated all of my concerns and anxieties. Dr. Neumann was the first to advise me that I may have to move or possibly find another line of work. He talked to me in a caring and compassionate manner. He was respectful in both his verbal and non-verbal communication. I didn't take offense to his mentioning of moving; I was able to see that as a possible solution. In fact, it reminded me of what I already knew.

I reflected on my attempts to join the Las Vegas Metropolitan Police Department. As soon I returned home, I was going to check the status of my application. I knew Las Vegas had a hiring freeze, but when would that be over? Would it be over in time to rescue me from this disaster?

Dr. Neumann concluded my appointment by recommending that I be placed on sick leave for 30 days. I thanked him and left his office after scheduling a follow-up appointment in a week.

On October 13, 2003, I arrived at the Detroit Police Medical Section and turned in the medical recommendation from Dr. Neumann. Sgt. Schmidt took it and told me that Dr. Rainey was out of town for a week. She warned me that I must complete the family leave act form in order to keep my healthcare benefits. She also informed me that I could not stay off work longer than the 12 weeks with the family medical leave, and I would have to use my banked sick time. When she asked me if I had any unused sick time, I told her yes, but not how much. I had a large amount of unused sick time, because during my nine years of service, I rarely called in sick.

Sgt. Carol Schmidt requested that I complete the medical release form for Dr. Neumann. Before I left, she reminded me that I must keep my October 23, 2003 appointment with Dr. Rainey.

I walked out of the office annoyed that I was expected to use my personal time and to file a family medical leave act. I never did complete that paperwork. I knew that my situation was duty-related and the department's responsibility.

A week later at 8:00 a.m., I received a call from Lt. Frazier stating that I must give more details about the stressful situation of October 4, 2003, the date of the robbery set-up. I had to complete a disability form and give it to him. The form wasn't filled out enough to provide him with the details that caused me to stop working. I wondered if this was just another means of harassment. Was he in on this too? My statement was limited to a small space on the form; I had room only for the following:

> Starting in July 2003, my supervisor advised me of several citizen complaints filed against me. Since I had not been named in citizen complaints in the past, it concerned me. I had always exhibited pride and professionalism in my work. I found that the complaints apparently were lodged against other officers. However, my supervisor disregarded the facts relayed by the complainant which should have clearly indicated that the accusations did not apply to me. Prior to this time, I had an exemplary record. It appeared to me that the supervisor was retaliating against me for my reporting to the Michigan State Police certain wrongful conduct by the mayor's staff.

On October 23, 2003, I arrived for my appointment at the Detroit Police Medical Section and again spoke to Sgt. Schmidt. She stated, "Dr. Rainey said you should go back to work!" She then asked if I had any available sick time or if I was ready to return to work.

I was adamant. "No! I'm not ready to return to work."

She declared that Dr. Neumann must send paperwork supporting his recommendation for sick leave. Since I had kept my follow-up appointments with Dr. Neumann, I felt confident that he would have no problem writing a report to the department to detail why I needed to stay off work. I received an appointment to return to the Detroit Police Medical Section in two weeks.

The next day, I realized that the department was going to try to force me back to work. I feared that once I returned, they would try to set me up again on some type of false criminal charges. Worse yet, I feared that in an attempt to retaliate against me, someone would cause me great bodily harm or try to kill me. I couldn't go back! I felt that the only way to protect myself was to get legal counsel. Therefore, on this day, I retained Michael L. Stefani of Troy, Michigan as my attorney. I needed him to investigate the harassment toward me by the City of Detroit under the Michigan Whistleblowers' Protection Act.

On October 27, I kept my scheduled appointment with Dr. Neumann and returned home.

At 12:00 p.m., I was at my residence, and the doorbell rang. I jumped up from my chair in the upstairs bedroom. I looked through the window blinds and saw Sgt. Weber from the 7th Precinct in full uniform. I lost confidence in the supervisors from the precinct, so I didn't deactivate the house alarm or answer the door. I watched as Weber scribbled something on paper and placed it in my mailbox. Later in the evening I retrieved it. The document was from the Detroit Police Department Internal Affairs Unit. It listed my rank, name, and badge number. It was an inter-office memorandum for a Garrity interview on November 7, 2003, at 6:30 a.m. about Investigation #03-219, the alleged armed robbery that occurred October 4, 2003 (the set-up).

❧    ☙

On November 3, 2003, I arrived an hour late to my appointment with Dr. Rainey. The receptionist informed me, "He's gone for the day." I asked her to let him know that I overslept and apologize for missing my appointment.

At 10:25 a.m., I met Sgt. Schmidt at the DPD Medical Section, and she mentioned my missed appointment with Dr. Rainey. I explained that I had been very drowsy and dozed off right before my appointment. At that time, I wasn't sleeping at night. I paced the floor, feeling that I had to watch over my wife and kids. I sat in a comfortable chair near the bedroom window that gave me a good view of the street. My house was the second one from the corner, so it was easy for me to see the side street too. I could watch any activity from several directions. I would steal "cat naps" in my chair while sitting vigil.

Was Dr. Rainey really gone for the day at 9:00 a.m. or did he not want to see me because I was late? I will never know for sure. I handed Sgt. Schmidt the etiology letter from Dr. Neumann that advised me to remain on sick leave for 30 days. She stated the print on Dr. Neumann's letter was too small for her to read.

"That letter is not for you to read; it's for Dr. Rainey."

She gave me a dirty look and scheduled an appointment for the following week. At that time, I was alternating appointments between the police department doctor, whom I didn't trust, with my personal physician, whom I did trust. I didn't mind what seemed to be weekly appointments. I was just concerned that the department was trying to force me to pay for the suffering they had caused. I was grateful that my doctor made sure that the department paid for what was clearly a duty-related "stress" injury. However, I was beginning to grow weary of the games that the department was playing. The administration continually tried to discover a way to force me back to work or to use my personal time.

On November 11, 2003, I told Officer Nelthrope that I thought the Detroit Police Department had me running around like a chicken with its head cut off. I was tired, frustrated, and felt something needed to be done. Nelthrope suggested that I talk it over with my attorney. I called attorney Michael Stefani at 3:10 p.m. and gave him full details of the Detroit Police Department's actions against me. He suggested that I wait and see where they were going with the allegation of the armed robbery. He also told me to bear with the doctor appointments until we could determine their focus. I was still hoping to receive help from the Detroit Police Officers Association (DPOA) or any other agency. Although I didn't reach out to them for help, I did hope that they would contact me, since my plight was now public. I don't harbor any ill feelings toward the DPOA nor do I think they were involved or condoned the harassment I received. I believe the union would have assisted me, if I had actually contacted a representative. However, at that moment I was unsure if I could trust anyone associated with the department.

"Let no man pull you low enough to hate him."
*Dr. Martin Luther King, Jr.*

On November 12, 2003, I reported at the Psychiatry Crisis Center, at 8:00 a.m., as directed by the DPD Medical Section. During this particular appointment, I immediately noticed that Dr. Rainey's attitude and personality was harsh. He opened the lobby door and demanded that I follow him. He walked swiftly and rigidly back toward his office. Once I sat down, he began to reprimand me about missing my last appointment. "The staff said you had an attitude when you arrived late for your appointment on November 3, 2003!"

I paused for a moment before I replied. "They are incorrect. I did not display an attitude on my last visit."

Dr. Rainey continued to shout very loudly. "You had an attitude with the staff!" He rambled on and on.

I started to smile and told myself he was trying to antagonize me for some apparent reason. That was when I discerned that he was following orders from the mayor's administration. Dr. Rainey then tried to put words into my mouth. "You are okay and should return to work, right?" He went on to affirm that 30 days off from work was enough time.

I retorted by stating that "30 days was not sufficient" and that Dr. Neumann was counseling me. I maintained that I was reaching a point where I could identify ways of dealing with the stress.

Dr. Rainey asked, "How is Dr. Neumann helping you?"

"He uses the tools of conversation and verbal therapy, unlike what you are doing by antagonizing me."

Dr. Rainey became quiet for a moment and then abruptly asked "What is it you do at home?"

I answered "I read, surf the Internet, and listen to talk radio."

"What is it your reading?"

"I read motivational, inspirational, and spiritual material."

He became still for an instant as if he were thinking deviously. "That's not good. You should return to work!" He asked how much I weighed.

I answered hesitantly, "I think 290 pounds. I'm really not sure, because I haven't run for two weeks." I told him I normally ran three miles, six days a week.

He then stated very boorishly, "That's not what you told me last time!" He shuffled vigorously through some paperwork. It appeared that he could not find what he wanted, so he jumped up and said, "Follow me," as he clearly displayed frustration that he couldn't bait me into an argument.

I followed him to an old rusty scale. I stood on it, and he roughly slid the weighted marker all the way to the end and shouted angrily, "295 pounds. You can leave now!" as he pointed to the door.

When I reached my car, I sat a moment and pondered what I believed was Dr. Rainey's sole purpose: to antagonize me into uncontrollable rage. I thought maybe he wanted me to act out of control. If I lost control and started yelling and screaming at him that would have given him probable cause to commit me to the psych ward. He became frustrated when his ploy failed repeatedly. I couldn't believe Dr. Rainey would stoop that low to fulfill the mayor's mission. I would not allow myself to hate Dr. Rainey, but I disliked what he was doing to me! As the Hippocratic Oath clearly shows, Dr. Rainey disregarded his sacred duty to care for me as his patient:

> Into whatever patient setting I enter, I will go for the benefit of the sick and will abstain from every voluntary act of mischief or corruption and further from the seduction of any patient...to keep this Oath unviolated may it be granted to me to enjoy life and the practice of the art and science of medicine with the blessing of the Almighty and respected by my peers and society,

but should I trespass and violate this Oath, may the reverse by my lot. — *The Hippocratic Oath (Modern Version)*

"You can discover what your enemy fears most
by observing the means he uses to frighten you."
*Eric Hoffer*

At 10:00 a.m., I arrived at the DPD Medical Section, as directed by Sgt. Schmidt. Before I met with her, a 7ᵗʰ Precinct sergeant I did not know approached me. He was African American, 5'9", dark complexion, bald, and. dressed in full uniform. He directed me to report to the IA Unit, per Sgt. Morgan Samuels. He advised me to report on November 16, 2003 at 6:30 a.m. on duty. The sergeant handed me the document and ordered me to endorse it. The document was a duplicate copy of the DPD inter-office memorandum from the IA Unit #03-219. After I signed the document, the sergeant turned and walked away.

Sgt. Schmidt asked me to step into her office. She quietly explained that the sergeant once worked in the medical section. She asked me to take a seat, as she nervously shuffled some papers on her desk. I was not prepared for what happened next; I was blindsided by the order!

Sgt. Schmidt directed me to turn in my weapon and report to work that night on restricted duty. I sat in my seat stunned, as I stared at the floor. I looked up and said, "They expect me to report to work on the desk at midnight with no weapon? You, they, the mayor are all crazy if you expect me to report for duty at midnight without a weapon."

She timidly said, "I understand your concern. They wanted me to serve you with the memorandum from IA. I told them no! Let someone else do it!"

I complied with her direct order and remove my .40 cal. Glock from my off-duty holster. I removed the magazine and the live round from the weapon. I left the slide open after checking to make sure the weapon was clear.

Sgt. Schmidt handed me a large envelope and asked me to place my weapon inside it.

Before leaving, I said, "I refuse to report to the 7th Precinct tonight!" I left the medical section without a weapon to defend myself. I was very concerned for my safety and felt that my life was in imminent danger. I now understood why Dr. Rainey told me that the staff said I had an attitude and why he continually tried to provoke me to anger in our meetings. He was trying to lay a false foundation to support his false diagnosis. His chief complaint for collecting my weapon was that I allegedly became hostile. Once my weapon was sequestered, I felt that the powers that be would arrange to have me murdered. I believed I had witnessed too much corruption in the Kilpatrick Administration.

"Wisdom is knowing what to do next; virtue is doing it."
*David Star Jordan*

I was frightened and felt like everybody had deserted me. I was all alone. I became frantic as I drove toward home, looking at every car and person who came near my vehicle. By the time I pulled into my driveway, I felt my heart pounding! My breathing was rapid, and my fists tightly grasped the steering wheel. Then suddenly I realized that tears were rolling down my cheeks. I quickly reverted to my training on how to handle a high stress call. I started to control my breathing and talk myself down. I truly thought I was losing it for the first time in my life.

When I was under control, I looked around to see if anyone had witnessed my breakdown. I wiped the tears from my eyes and shook my head a couple of times. I never shared that awkward moment with anyone, not even my wife. I felt it was important for her to see me stay strong in this situation. She was already beginning to show her emotions over this ordeal and I didn't want to add any stress to her and the kids.

In the house, I immediately called my attorney, Michael Stefani, and told him that Mayor Kilpatrick's latest tactic was the final straw. I explained in full detail the events that occurred from Dr. Rainey's appointment through Sgt. Schmidt's order confiscating of my duty weapon.

Stefani asked if I was ready for a press conference to announce that I was suing the City of Detroit, the Detroit Police Department, Chief Jerry Oliver, and Mayor Kwame Kilpatrick. Stefani was set to investigate and pursue any viable legal claim for harassment directed toward me as a result of my protected activity under the Michigan Whistleblowers' Protection Act. I told Stefani that it was definitely the right time.

# Mayor accused of getting even

## *Whistle-blowing ex-bodyguard sues Kilpatrick*

### By BEN SCHMITT
FREE PRESS STAFF WRITER

One of Mayor Kwame Kilpatrick's former most trusted bodyguards accused the mayor Thursday of leading a conspiracy to ruin his career as retaliation for going public with allegations against members of the executive security team.

Detroit Police Officer Walter Harris, 38, said Kilpatrick is out to destroy him because Harris went public with allegations of overtime fraud, drunken driving and cover-ups of auto accidents by the mayor's security team.

Harris sued the mayor, former Police Chief Jerry Oliver and the City of Detroit on Thursday under the Michigan Whistleblowers' Protection Act. He has been on

RASHAUN RUCKER/Detroit Free Press

**Detroit Police Officer Walter Harris has been on sick leave since early October.**

sick leave since early October, citing stress and depression.

Kilpatrick's spokesman Howard Hughey declined comment Thursday on the lawsuit.

Harris' lawsuit, filed Thursday

*Please see* HARRIS, Page 3A

# Officer in probe of mayor files suit

## Ex-bodyguard says he was targeted after he testified about Kilpatrick and other cops.

By Darci McConnell
*The Detroit News*

**DETROIT** — A police officer who told state investigators that he witnessed wrongful acts by Mayor Kwame Kilpatrick and his bodyguards sued the city on Thursday, saying he has since been the target of a campaign to discredit his reputation.

**Harris**

**Stefani**

Officer Walt Harris, a former member of Mayor Kwame Kilpatrick's bodyguard unit, filed a lawsuit against the city of Detroit, Kilpatrick and former Detroit Police Chief Jerry A. Oliver Sr. The suit claims police officials, at the direction of Kilpatrick and Oliver, steered and fabricated citizen complaints

**Kilpatrick**

**Oliver**

# Mayor: I'm solo on late-night outings

## *Kilpatrick denies cheating on his wife*

**By JIM SCHAEFER AND M.L. ELRICK**
FREE PRESS STAFF WRITERS

Kwame Kilpatrick said former bodyguards were wrong about driving him to affairs with other women.

Detroit Mayor Kwame Kilpatrick admitted this week in a lawsuit deposition that he sometimes ditches his bodyguards for late-night solo drives through "the city that gave me so much," but denied several allegations that he cheated on his wife.

"I roll down the windows and have time with Kwame in Detroit," Kilpatrick testified Monday, according to a transcript the Free Press obtained Friday. "I see some of the projects that we need to get done. ... I see some of the things that my directors tell me they've gotten done, and I go by those different things.

"But I like being with the city by myself, because this is the city that gave me so much."

Former police bodyguard Walt Harris testified in a deposition earlier this year that Kilpatrick's nighttime forays had more to do with extramarital dalliances. Kilpatrick's testimony contradicted Harris, who has a separate lawsuit against the city.

*Please see* **MAYOR, Page 10A**

He advised me that the press conference would be held in his office on November 13, 2003. After the call, I contacted Officer Nelthrope and put him on notice about the press conference. I shared with him that I felt like I was in that 1970 police movie "Serpico."

I then contacted my mother and informed her of my decision. She was dismayed that I had to put my trust in an attorney, because I trusted no law enforcement agency. I really had no background information on Stefani, other than the fact that he was representing Officer Nelthrope and Gary Brown. Attorney Stefani appeared to be the only person on Earth that was not afraid of Mayor Kilpatrick.

At 4:00 p.m., I called the 7th Precinct and advised the duty sergeant that I was sick and would not report for duty that night. Later that evening, I sat down with my wife, who had just arrived at home from work. I explained to her that it was time to take action. Surely if whistleblowers suffer reprisals for speaking out, the solution must be the laws that protect whistleblowers. I told her that Mayor Kilpatrick had left me no option; I must file a lawsuit against the city under the Michigan Whistleblower Protection Act. Knowing they had taken my weapon and assigned me to work midnights unarmed, my wife was in total agreement with me. She became very afraid not only for my safety but for the kids as well.

> "I must confess that since the first time
> I heard myself referred to as a whistleblower,
> I cringed, and I am still uneasy with that term.
> It sounds demeaning. Demeaning for so noble a cause."
> *Serpico*

On November 13, 2003, after not having slept the night before, I prepped my clothes for the afternoon press conference. I pulled out my dark suit with the French blue pin stripes and a French blue shirt. I grabbed my gold and French blue tie and made sure my shoes were brightly polished. I saw my wife to the door and kissed her goodbye as she left for work. Later, I dropped my children off at my mother's house so that I could finish preparing for the press conference.

When I arrived at home, I discovered two very large dead rats, one each at my front and rear doors. I first thought to contact the police and file a report. I overruled my emotions and elected not to call. I removed both of the dead rats and discarded them in the trash.

Inside, I asked myself what in the hell was happening and if I was doing what was best for the family. After spending some quiet time alone, I showered and changed my clothes for the press conference.

I drove to attorney Stefani's office with my head on a swivel, watching for any impending danger. Approaching his building, I saw various news media trucks. Before I entered, I thought about telling Stefani about the dead rats. My major concern was who did it: other officers or Kilpatrick's henchmen. Should I be concerned that someone believed I was wrong for talking and labeled me a "rat?" Was it simply a scare tactic to keep me from saying anything more? I decided to keep it to myself and not alert my adversaries that I was afraid.

I walked inside Stefani's office and strolled past reporters I had often encountered while working for Mayor Kilpatrick. I met with Stefani who asked if I was ready. I assured him that I was. While waiting for more news reporters to arrive, I read an article on the wall in the kitchen of Stefani's office. It indicated that Stefani was a former FBI agent and a member of the Detroit Police Department. I observed some pictures on the wall that supported the article. This is when I realized I was in good hands and why Stefani was not troubled by Kilpatrick or his inner circle. Stefani became my hero, and I placed my full trust in him.

The press conference started at 1:15 p.m., and Mayor Kwame Kilpatrick, Chief Jerry Oliver, and the City of Detroit were placed on notice about the lawsuit.

> "If a friend is in trouble, don't annoy him by asking
> if there is anything you can do.
> Think up something appropriate and do it."
> *Edgar Watson Howe*

The day following the press conference started off with a pleasant surprise. I picked up the Detroit News and saw an article written by Darci McConnell. It ended with a statement from the former mayor, Dennis Archer:

Archer said Thursday that Harris was "outstanding" as his bodyguard. "He was well-respected by his colleagues, and I had the utmost respect for his professionalism and service."

I very much appreciated Mayor Archer's remarks. After the news of the lawsuit aired on all local TV news stations and appeared in the newspapers, I received a voice mail message. The call came from a former member of Mayor Archer's EPU. The officer said, "I saw the press conference, and I've got your back." I will never forget that message. The only reason I didn't return his call was because I did not want to have any other officer's career ruined. I was so concerned that there was a tap on my phone and didn't want to implicate him.

Another officer from Archer's EPU called and asked if I needed any money. He said that he had approximately eight or nine hundred dollars that he could withdrawal from the bank if I needed it. Even though I could have used the money, I told him I was okay. I did not borrow the money because sometimes money breaks up friendships. I certainly would have paid my debt, but it would have been a matter of time. I was honored to know that these men would come to my help at any moment if I needed them. I was touched by the offer to help financially, knowing what the sacrifice would have meant to him.

Those were the only officers from the previous unit who called to show their solidarity. This meant a lot to me, as I knew in that moment they were true friends.

"A hyena cannot smell its own stench."
*Kalenjin Kenya*

A few days after the press conference, I observed a Michigan Bell telephone truck parked outside my house, always two houses away. I became aware that my home phone began to click uncontrollably. Then there was static to the point where I would have to call the person back. Callers always became annoyed by the clicking and asked if it was my phone.

One day from my back deck, I saw a Michigan Bell lineman up on the telephone pole. When my wife returned home from work, I asked her about the telephone truck parked outside.

"I was wondering if you noticed that truck too," she said.

I told her that I truly believed that Kilpatrick and his cronies were tapping our line. She didn't want to believe it, because it seemed more like something from a movie and not something that was happening to us! Finally I told family members and friends, "If you want to share sensitive information over the phone, please call me on my cell."

During that same time, I noticed various automobiles following me. They appeared to be unmarked city cars driven by different men and women. This type of surveillance almost became a game of cat and mouse. I would engage in evasive driving and lose the vehicles. I never confronted the drivers, giving them a reason to use lethal force.

The harassment then escalated to people following me on foot, even when shopping in the suburbs. At times during this torment I thought I was becoming paranoid. That was until Kilpatrick's henchmen began to get sloppy in their tactics. It was becoming evident to others that people were watching and following me.

The intimidation became bolder. One particular day, my wife asked me to pick up some groceries while she was at work. I decided to go to a nearby supermarket in Grosse Pointe. It was a cool morning; I was dressed in a sweatshirt and blue jeans. While shopping, I noticed an African American man watching me. I entered the checkout lane and continued to notice this man following and watching me. After I paid for my groceries, I proceeded to leave the store. Just as I pushed my grocery cart toward the door to exit the store, the Black man came running toward me. He was still in the store but behind the checkout lanes. He jumped over the chain that closed off one lane and intercepted me at the door.

I immediately took a defensive stance and came within seconds of kicking him in the chest.

"Hey, man, I mean no harm," as he threw his hands up and smiled. "Don't you get cold in just a sweatshirt on your morning jogs? I would wear a bulletproof vest." He turned and hastily walked away, without ever turning back to look at me.

I proceeded to my vehicle with my head on swivel, checking for an ambush. I quickly used my training and checked my vehicle for a car bomb. Once I cleared it, I loaded my groceries and rapidly left the parking lot. On the way home, I took an alternate route and continued to check my rearview mirrors. There was no doubt that I was in condition red, fully alert.

Once I arrived home, I checked the outer perimeter for any signs of trouble. I unloaded the groceries and thought about the encounter at the store. Why did that guy approach me and make the remark about me jogging in a sweatshirt? The comment about wearing a bulletproof vest, was it a threat on my life? I believed Kilpatrick was making me aware that I was being watched and that he knew my daily schedule. I was again running three miles on Outer Drive Avenue every day at 6:00 a.m. Although my routine had been interrupted by the stress of recent events, I had returned to running in hopes that it would help me to relieve some of the stress of my situation.

After receiving that threat on my life, I knew that reporting it to the police was not an option. I trusted no one in law enforcement; in fact, I often felt that if I would be murdered, it could be by a police officer.

Earlier in the year, I saw the news reports about Tamara Greene's murder. Tamara "Strawberry" Greene became Detroit's murder victim #113 on April 30, 2003. The local newspapers reported that she had been shot approximately 18 times with a .40 caliber weapon while in the driver's seat of a parked car. The rumors began to run rampant that Greene had danced at the rumored Manoogian Mansion party. It was also rumored that she had been beaten by Carlita Kilpatrick. At this point in my life with the harassment and intimidation, I recalled the story of the stripper. I asked myself the question: Is this the method used to silence those who could talk? .

I really became more uneasy about my own security and almost felt like I needed to go underground. After realizing the depth of my exposure to city hall corruption, I truly believed that I could end up a victim in an unsolved murder case. I was afraid that my children would be left without a father and my wife without the love of her life.

At this juncture, I sensed that the only way to survive was to tell almost everything I knew about the corruption. I believed that any harm brought on after my testimony would most certainly illuminate the Kilpatrick Administration. I believed they tried to have me arrested and jailed with the bogus armed robbery. Once that failed, I was absolutely convinced that, to keep me quiet, they would kill me. I was very afraid for my personal safety and that of my family.

I failed to mention the supermarket incident to my wife, because I didn't want to scare her and cause her to worry more about me and the safety of our family. I wanted to present her with a positive plan of action. I wanted to be able to say, "Honey, I have some good news and bad news. The bad news is…." I couldn't see any good news in this situation at all. I knew that it would only be bad, very bad news for her. She already was feeling the stress of my situation. I had hoped I could keep it from her to spare her undue worry, in the hope that all would be well again soon. Unfortunately, that wasn't the case.

I wasn't able to keep it from her for long. The next event of intimidation occurred while I was out with my family. One Saturday evening in November, my family and I met Officer Hamilton and his family at Eastland Mall. My wife's birthday was quickly approaching, and I wanted to buy her something from Macy's. My partner and I persuaded the wives and kids to go look around inside the mall.

At Macy's, I wanted to purchase a Coach™ purse that my wife wanted. I was looking at purses in the glass case, when I felt someone staring at me. I looked up and across the room observed a tall white man watching me. My partner immediately said, "Yeah, Walt, he's watching you. There is a Black woman with him too."

I looked for the Black woman but could not find her. After I completed my purchase, I told my partner, "Let's go into the mall and do some counter-surveillance."

Just as we entered the mall, I called my wife on my cell. Without going into detail, I told her to meet me in front of Macy's immediately.

My wife arrived somewhat frantic, asking what was going on. I explained that some people had been watching me, and we needed to leave right away. I gave her instructions, once we walked outside the mall, to get the car while I stood by with the children. My partner added, "I got your back; my Glock is loaded."

We moved outside, and I watched my wife as she quickly walked to our vehicle. Our families were standing together in the cold with six small children.

My wife entered our car, which was parked nearby, and suddenly the tall white male walked past us. He walked approximately 10 feet away and stopped on the sidewalk. He put his cell to his ear and appeared to be talking. My partner stated "Don't worry, doc, I got your back. Let him make a wrong move."

I loaded my children into our vehicle, slid behind the wheel, and pulled over to my partner's vehicle until his family was inside their car. The man was still standing outside as we left the parking lot. My partner followed us and stood by until we were inside the house.

After my wife bathed the children and put them to bed, I told her we needed to talk. She was nervous and upset about what had happened in the mall, and I knew it was time to reveal what was going on. I told her that people had been following me in vehicles and on foot. It was not a case of paranoia, because my partner saw it at the mall. I informed her that the police department had confiscated my weapon and launched an attack to terrorize me. "We have to pack up and move out of state before somebody gets hurt!"

She was obviously upset and had mixed emotions about leaving our home. We sat in the breakfast nook talking for hours. She cried and I held her hand while I fought back tears. We even found a way to laugh. By finding an ounce of humor in the situation, it became a moment of therapy as we moved forward to a solution. As the early dawn light peaked through the window, we were in complete agreement. Leaving Detroit was in our family's best interest. Life was about to change for our family, but what mattered most is that we would all be safe and together.

Next we discussed a plan of action. Where would we go? How would we survive if we were both unemployed? I said that I would call Sheriff Stephen Sharp, who was the chief of police when I was an officer for the City of Bloomington (1991-1993). Furthermore, my wife and I agreed to consult with the pastor of our church for guidance. She later told me she had already gone to our pastor for counseling on how to handle our situation. We both knew that we had to leave Detroit, but we were not sure where to go. My wife would have to leave her new job, and I would have to resign from the department. My wife hoped that we could stay somewhere in Michigan, so she could commute to work. Her concern was how we would support our children if we were both out of work and relocating out of state.

# Chapter 13

# Relocate for Safety

"Anyone can give up;
it's the easiest thing in the world to do.
But to hold it together when
everyone else would understand
if you fell apart, that's true strength."
*Unknown*

One Monday morning in early November 2003, I called Sheriff Sharp. He was out of town on training and would not return for a week. While I waited to hear back from him, I needed to seek guidance from my pastor.

My 7th Precinct partner went to the church with me. I told my pastor in great detail what I had witnessed since I left the mayor's office: the set-up at the precinct with the bogus armed robbery and citizens' complaints; the police department doctor having my duty weapon confiscated and ordering me back to work unarmed on the midnight shift; the press conference announcing the lawsuit; my home phone being tapped; people following me in cars and on foot; and my concern for the safety of my family and how I would provide for them.

My pastor stated, first of all, that we needed to pray and ask God for guidance. After praying, he said he had read the newspapers and knew about some of the circumstances. He strongly suggested that I move out from under the thumb of the City of Detroit. The mayor and the police department controlled my paycheck and insurance.

Basically they controlled my life at that point. My pastor recommended that I resign and leave Michigan. He also asked if I had a particular state and job in mind. I mentioned that I was in the process of contacting Sheriff Sharp in Indiana. My pastor thought that was good and asked me to keep him informed on what I decided to do. This was the confirmation I needed to know: God had a plan for me and my family.

"In skating over thin ice, our safety is in our speed."
*Ralph Waldo Emerson*

I called Sheriff Sharp in Bloomington again. We exchanged pleasantries and then I asked if he had any job openings. "Walt, you can start tomorrow if you want. You're a good guy!"

"Sheriff Sharp, I really appreciate that but before I go any further, let me explain my circumstances." I went into detail about the whistleblower lawsuit and the mayor's office. After explaining everything to the sheriff, he said, "Unfortunately, this happens to a lot of good cops. They are blackballed for telling the truth. Walter, if you would like to work here, I have a job for you! When do you want to start?"

He recommended that I come to Bloomington and tour the facility. He remembered my wife, and I told him that we now had three young children. "Great," he said. "You and your family should come on down and if you like what I have to offer, give me a starting date."

With a joyful voice, I told him I would like to take him up on his offer and made plans to meet with him on December 10, 2003. When I turned the phone off, I recall saying, "Thank you, Jesus. God does answer prayer." This underscored how important it is to have good work ethic and integrity and to always leave a job in good standing.

I told my wife the good news, and she was moved to tears. She loved living in Bloomington and was relieved that at least one of us would have a job when we got there. We made a family decision to move back to Indiana, and we did not waver.

On December 9, 2003, I packed our RV and drove to the post office down the street from my house. My RV is 30 feet long and takes up two parking spaces, so I pulled up in front of the post office, alongside the mail boxes. My wife went inside to purchase some stamps and mail some bill payments before we left town.

I got out of the car and walked to the back of the RV to check on the kids. I heard someone knock on the front passenger window. It was an African American woman. "How can I help you?" I asked.

She smiled. "Mr. Officer, next time you might not want to park in front of the mailboxes." She then turned and walked away and entered a vehicle which appeared to be city-owned. When my wife returned to the RV, I asked her if she had talked to anyone inside. She said she spoke only with the mail clerk who sold her the stamps.

"You didn't speak to a Black woman inside?" I asked angrily.

My wife snapped back, "I didn't talk to anyone. Who was that woman at the window?"

"I believe it was one of Kilpatrick's watchdogs again." I told her we had to move out of state quickly. Kilpatrick's people were becoming bolder. The woman who tapped on my RV window let me know that she knew who I was and where I was located. That was another attempt to intimidate and cause me to lash out. We left the post office and jumped on I-94 West.

> "You know where you have been,
> but you don't know where you will end up in life."
> *Gloria Harris*

Approximately 50 miles south of Indianapolis, Bloomington is the home of Indiana University. A college town seemed to be a safe and civil place to relocate my family and start over. I knew it would be a safe place to raise my children. My wife and I were well-known from the years we spent there as students and from my past work in law enforcement. We had several close friends there to turn to for comfort. People knew me and my character. We had so many good memories and wanted to return to a place that had been a positive time in our lives.

I felt that moving to Bloomington would give my family a chance to recover from the stress and emotional pain of leaving our home in Detroit. With our house on the market, we had to find an apartment. The children would have to leave a home with plenty of space and adjust living in an apartment with limited room to play.

I arrived a day early for my meeting with Sheriff Sharp and decided to check out some apartments. Once we narrowed our apartment search down to two, we decided to wait for the job confirmation.

Later in the evening, we had dinner with a Bloomington couple we had known for years. During dinner conversation, the husband said to me, "I want to tell you something in private." We walked to the rear of the restaurant, away from both families. He told me that earlier that day someone called him at 3:00 a.m. and said "I'm going to kill you, motherfucker." He said that his wife was not able to sleep because of that phone call. The family had never before received that type of threatening phone call.

This confirmed that my phone line in Detroit was tapped. I apologized to my friend if the phone call he received exposed his family to threats. He and his family were frightened after being told why we were relocating. This situation, I believe, put a strain on our friendship. After we moved back to Bloomington, we had very little contact with them. To this very day, we seldom communicate, sadly, after more than 20 years of friendship.

On December 10, 2003, I met with Sheriff Sharp and toured the facilities. I saw some old and new faces at the Monroe County Correctional Facility. The sheriff introduced me to all the staff and said that I would be working there soon. He also told them that once a road deputy position opened, I would fill it. I looked at him and said, "I guess that means I accept the job."

I gave Sheriff Sharp the starting date of December 20, 2003. I hugged him and thanked him for helping me and my family. We ate lunch together at a local restaurant. During that time, he informed me that the Bloomington Police Department would begin hiring the next month. The pay and the benefits were better than what the county offered. Since Sheriff Sharp was serving his last term, he suggested that I check into the city's hiring process. "Walt, you don't have to inquire with the city, if you don't want to."

I had a family, so of course the pay and benefits were important to me. According to the Indiana Law Enforcement Training Council, I was still certified as a police officer in the State of Indiana.

After completing our lunch, we walked back to the Monroe County Correctional Facility. We ran into Captain Jeff Buchanan of the Bloomington Police Department. Sheriff Sharp told him I was moving back to Bloomington, working at the county. Captain Buchanan shook my hand and invited me to apply to the Bloomington Police Department in January.

My wife and I secured an apartment and a mailbox at the post office. We returned to Detroit and began planning our exit strategy. I reserved a U-Haul truck with a car hitch and purchased some boxes. I summoned help from two of my closest friends, but they made excuses why they could not help me load the truck.

I planned to submit my resignation to the Detroit Police Department on December 15 and move out in the middle of the night of December 17, 2003.

"Everything in life requires a price.
Know how much you're willing to pay."
*Anonymous*

Early the next morning, I walked into the 7th Precinct and went to the police officers' report room. I located a resignation/retirement notification form and sat down at the typewriter. I completed the form even though the typewriter was in poor condition, causing me to make errors which I tried to correct.

I walked down to Commander Riley McCarthy's office and knocked on the door; he told me to enter. I introduced myself, because he was new to the precinct as of October 15. I presented my resignation and waited for his endorsement. I wrote the following as my reason for resigning:

> I am leaving due to the unsafe, unprofessional work environment of the Detroit Police Department; specifically the 7th Precinct and the mayor's staff. I was called by the state police to give statements in the investigation of the mayor's staff. I spoke about wrongful acts by certain members of the mayor's staff. Since that time, I have been harassed and retaliated against at the precinct level. I no longer feel safe at work. I fear for my family's safety. Therefore, I must leave the Detroit Police Department and Detroit, Michigan.

Immediately after I resigned, I proceeded to move my family to Bloomington. For the safety and security of my wife and kids, we moved during the night! We pulled the moving truck in front of the house and moved only what we could carry during the night-time hours. My friend from Michigan City, Indiana and my precinct partner came to help, and several family members came by to say their goodbyes.

It was a very stressful time for my wife and me. We had a fair share of arguments over what to take and what to leave behind. Many of our things were given to our church, family, and friends, but the bulk of items were left in the garage. We needed to leave the house empty, so that the realtor could sell it.

Just before 2 a.m., I hitched my vehicle to the moving truck for towing to Indiana. As I walked through my house with my oldest son for the last time, I stopped in the doorway. Before locking the front door, I told my son, who was six and a half, to remember that day. I told him that we were forced to move out of town, because Daddy was a police officer and told the truth.

We pulled away from our house, and my wife said, "Remember Lot's wife (from the Bible) and never look back." I thought the move reminded me more of the people of Egypt, whom Moses led across the Red Sea to safety. The people escaped the evil pharaoh and his army with the help of God.

We had moved so stealthily that even our neighbors didn't realize we were gone. It wasn't until several days later that the neighbors noticed the house stayed dark and they didn't see our cars. They decided to use our driveway so that it would not seem obvious to the public that the house was vacant.

I was happy that I could move my family safely from Detroit, yet at the same time I was sad to see us lose our first family home. We had lived in that house for more than eight years and had a lot of memories there, including bringing our three children home from the hospital.

❧   ☙

Everything happened so quickly. Before Christmas 2003, I was working for the sheriff's department and living in Indiana. My wife wasn't working, so she was able to stay at home with the children. It would take her months to find a new job in her field. Nevertheless, we were settling in well and starting to recover from the hasty move out of Detroit.

Within weeks of relocating to Indiana, one morning I was driving into work. I exited Highway 37 at Third Street and pulled into the McDonald's parking lot. I stopped because I noticed the front end of my car was handling strangely. Just as I was maneuvering a turn into the parking lot, my left front tire fell off. I was horrified, imagining my soft top Jeep Wrangler flipping over at 55 mph. I believed immediately that this was the work of the Kilpatrick Administration.

I called Mr. Stefani and explained the circumstances, and he advised me to make a police report. I followed his recommendation. After the tow truck driver arrived and assessed the front end, he said that someone had loosened the lugs manually.

Over the next months, there were no more unsettling incidents and again I began to feel more comfortable. During this time, I received word that the Bloomington Police Department had started their hiring process. I talked to Sheriff Sharp, and he encouraged me to make a move to the police department. I did, in fact, need the extra income and benefits package that the city had to offer.

Before applying, I met with Chief Michael Hostetler for at least half an hour in his office. When I told him I wanted to return to the police department, he said in his signature soft-spoken voice, "Walt, I told you when you left, you could always come back. You did an excellent job when you worked here before."

I left his office with a great sense of pride in having done my job well when I worked for the department a few years earlier. I picked up the application on my way out and spoke to one of the recruiting officers. I was extremely excited and a bit nervous about the process.

Even with the chief's support, I had to complete the entire hiring process, which was only fair. I'm sure it was required in order for me to receive approval of the police, civilian, and pension boards. The process included a written exam and a physical fitness test. In addition, I had to be cleared by a physician and a psychologist.

Once I was physically and mentally cleared, I still had to sit before a review board of police officers and then civilians. While I was interviewed by the police board, consisting of several officers, I was asked why I left Detroit. I was forthcoming with all the details of what happened. I even shared with them various newspaper clippings that I had brought with me. I spared no details in answering their many questions.

When the process was complete and my application was approved by both the police and civil boards, I was hired by the Bloomington Police Department. I was sworn in May 2004 by Mayor Mark Kruzan, and Chief Hostetler handed me my new badge. Later that evening, I celebrated with my wife and family celebrated at our favorite restaurant.

Walter Harris with Mayor Mark Kruzan, City Hall, 2004
Bloomington Police Department

Walter Harris shakes hands with Police Chief Michael Hostetler
Bloomington Police Department swearing-in, 2004

Walter Harris in full uniform, proud to be a public servant
Bloomington Police Department, 2004

I enjoyed patrolling Bloomington so much that, at times, I thought I was retired "on duty." There was less crime and fewer crime-provoking conditions than I faced in Detroit. Nevertheless, there were still the potential dangers that any police officer's job could bring. I missed my old partner. In Detroit, the officers patrol in pairs. In Bloomington, the officers rode alone. I didn't have anyone to talk to while out on patrol in the squad car. That took some getting used to; I had forgotten that aspect of the job.

Shortly after I joined the department, an incident occurred that quickly reminded me of my whistleblower situation. One night while driving to work a midnight shift, my brakes failed and I lost control of my vehicle during a turn and almost crashed. I contacted a local garage to tow and repair my brakes. The inspection showed a severed brake line. I filed a police report about the incident.

I was disheartened to believe that Kilpatrick's henchmen had followed me to Bloomington. I tried to put as many safety measures in place for my family. Many of the officers that I worked with were aware of what happened in Detroit. They were very supportive.

As the months turned into years, there were no further incidents of intimidation or harassment. We were moving forward with our lives and tried to enjoy all that Bloomington had to offer. My wife found a job that she absolutely loved. We attended many football games, tailgated, and reminisced about the good old days. Even my oldest son enjoyed Bloomington by participating in youth league football.

I was also very fortunate to have the chance to pay into my pension to make up for the lost years while I worked in Detroit. I was informed that if I paid into the retirement fund, I could gain the seniority I had lost. This wasn't seniority within the department but in the eyes of the pension board for future retirement eligibility. This later turned out to be a blessing in disguise.

# Chapter 14

# Whistleblower Cases

*"It's not the load that breaks you down; it's the way you carry it."*
*Lena Horne*

Mayor Kilpatrick used a multitude of lawyers and hired spokespersons at the taxpayers' expense. These hired guns were used to discredit me in any and every way. For instance, Attorney Samuel McCargo stated during a deposition that I left the mayor's security detail, because I was nervous. No, I voluntarily transferred out of the unit, because I witnessed corruption on a daily basis.

Attorney Valerie A. Colbert-Osamuede attempted to confuse me during a deposition about how long it took to drive to the UAW Family Education Center, Onaway, Michigan. She then tried to vigorously convince me that Mayor Kilpatrick and Christine Beatty occupied different hotel rooms while there. I continually corrected Mrs. Colbert-Osamuede that I witnessed the mayor remove his shirt and Christine Beatty remove her shoes while sitting on the bed in the same room. I then explained how Mayor Kilpatrick kicked everyone out the room except Christine Beatty.

Spokesman Howard Hughey stated, "Individuals making these salacious allegations want money, and they'll say or do anything to get that. It's a travesty."

Mayor Kilpatrick consistently called me a liar, when asked about my statements to the press or deposition. When I transferred to the 7th Precinct, I became inundated with false citizen complaints. The last artificial complaint, a robbery set-up, was meant for me. It was thwarted, because of an in-car camera installation that I demanded. Public officials will not falter in breaking laws, policies, or procedures to conceal embarrassing evidence. No one wants to believe a public official can be so corrupt.

Being in such a high-profile case made me unemployable in the State of Michigan. My phone line was being tapped, and strangers were following me on a daily basis. It was not until my life was threatened at the Farmer Jack's store that I realized I was in too deep. When there is much at stake, it's not unusual to receive death threats. My friends stopped calling, and I became isolated from members of the police department.

As I waited for my case to go to trial, I also waited for additional officers who witnessed the same corruption to come forward; however, it never happened. I was left with only one choice and that was to leave Michigan. I felt forced to resign and move out of state. By this time my finances, friends, and mental state were at an all time low. I lost my home and most of my possessions. I eventually lost my rental property and just about all my finances. I momentarily began to feel guilty for telling the truth because I also felt that everything my family went through was my fault. Yet, I knew I had to be a warrior and stand strong for my family.

I started life over at age 38 from scratch but if you had just met me, you would have never known. I drew strength from God, my mother, my wife, my pastor, the words from my coaches, and one of my closet friends.

"What was hard to endure is sweet to recall."
*Continental proverb*

In February 2004, shortly after we settled into the apartment in Bloomington, I began receiving calls from attorney Stefani about providing a deposition in the Nelthrope-Brown case. He made sure I knew upfront that the deposition was for their case. Even though I didn't really know Gary Brown, Nelthrope was my friend, and they both were my brothers in blue. I assured Stefani that I understood I was just a witness in their case. I believe he found it unusual for a witness in someone else's case to request time off from work, drive five hours, and also be responsible for all expenses. I felt it was the right thing to do. I was working, but I was struggling financially.

I went to Michigan on February 4, 2004. I avoided going into the Detroit city limits and met Stefani at his office in Royal Oak. I provided him the truth as I knew it. He again informed me that the deposition was for the Nelthrope-Brown case, not mine. At times during the deposition, Mr. Stefani would ask the stenographer to stop for awhile. During the breaks, the stenographer would whisper to me that she was anticipating the restart. It appeared that my testimony was so revealing that I left her hanging at the breaks. The stenographer by all means remained professional as she carried out her duty.

At any point during our meeting, Stefani would ask me, "How is it you know the mayor and Beatty had an intimate relationship?" I never lied to him or embellished what I witnessed; I merely stated the facts. In this case, I simply told him about their constantly texting each other with Skypager® during non-office hours. Stefani would say, "Say that again." And I would say, "Mayor Kilpatrick and Christine Beatty constantly texted each other on their Skypager® units."

I explained to Stefani that many times they texted each other late in the evening or night and often early in the morning. Several times they communicated during business trips. Often, after Kilpatrick texted, he would make a comment that he wasn't ready to leave the chauffeured city vehicle. He was slow to exit the vehicle, because he needed to "console Christine." He would make the comment that Christine and her husband were having marital problems.

Also, there were several times at the end of the day when he would make a phone call to Christine. He would say, "I will meet you in 10 minutes." He would tell security that he was done for the day and enter his home or the mansion. However, before we could pack up and leave or settle in the security room, he would rush from the back of the house and commandeer the city vehicle and speed out of the driveway. We would try to tell him to wait or that he shouldn't go alone, but he would not hear of it.

I was able to give Mr. Stefani several incidences that gave me the impression with certainty that there must have been more than a business relationship between the mayor and Christine. I also gave information about out-of-town hotel meetings between them.

I believe that the various conversations I had with my attorney about the intimate relationship of Kilpatrick and Beatty provided him with evidence. He must have realized that the truth and proof of what I was telling him resided in those text messages. If retrieved, they could provide proof of their relationship. I have no idea when exactly Stefani acquired the text messages, and I have never seen them outside of their exposure in the media after the case was over.

> "It's hard to believe that a man is telling
> the truth when you know that
> you would lie if you were in his place."
> *Henry Louis Mencken*

It wasn't until the Nelthrope-Brown case was completely over and settled that Mr. Stefani finally said to me over the telephone, "Everything you told me was the truth." I most certainly did not sensationalize any of my testimony in his deposition or to the Michigan State Police-attorney general's investigation which started during the closing stage of my career as a Detroit police officer.

Mayor Kilpatrick and his spokesperson had called me a liar. I felt that most of the department police officers and the public believed Kilpatrick and his administration. The depiction that I was a liar was painful to me and my family during the whistleblower ordeal.

I believe that Mr. Stefani did not realize how much my integrity meant to me during this tribulation. Maybe most attorneys are used to their clients stretching the truth or lying. Whenever I spoke with Stefani, I gave him the facts. I would go into great detail to make sure nothing important was left out.

Here is a quote that explains why I always spoke truthfully:

> "One smidgen of falsehood, fallacy, or overstatement from
> a whistleblower cancels a truckload of truth, logic, and accuracy."
> *Bill Corcoran*

I believe that Mr. Stefani played a very strategic game of chess in matters concerning my case. It started with missing a settlement court date. The settlement conference date in my case was adjourned twice. The first time was at the request of the defendants. In the second instance, on February 17, 2005, counsel for both parties appeared at the scheduled settlement conference. However, because the judge apparently was ill that day, the settlement conference date was rescheduled by the trial court to March 31, 2005.

Owing to confusion over several previous adjournments of the settlement conference date and also the rescheduling of a summary disposition hearing date, Mr. Stefani inadvertently failed to attend the settlement conference. Despite the fact that he had attended the previous settlement conference, which the judge missed due to illness, the judge, without a motion or prompting of any kind on the part of defendants' counsel, ruled from the bench and dismissed my lawsuit.

He dismissed it, because Mr. Stefani failed to appear on my behalf. This is where I had to wonder: Was it because of circumstances or was it a very well thought-out maneuver (very smart)?

I was disappointed to hear of the dismissal, yet I wanted to trust my attorney and believe that it was simply an oversight. I believed Stefani strategically missed the court date in hopes that he would get it reinstated. This would have allowed for my testimony to be heard in Nelthrope-Brown's case. If my case was settled prior to their case ever going to court, then it is very probable that the city would require me to become silent or the judge would issue a gag order regarding my testimony as part of a settlement.

Several journalists called me in Indiana, expecting me to be upset with the ruling. I did not express any anger; I explained to them that I forgave Mayor Kilpatrick and that I was trying to move on with my life. My family had sustained a significant financial loss, and my name and reputation had been tarnished. I was known as a liar against Mayor Kilpatrick and the city.

On April 12, 2005, Stefani filed a motion on my behalf asking the judge to set aside the order of dismissal and reinstate my lawsuit. He apologized to the trial court for his failure to attend the March 31, 2005 settlement conference and implored the judge not to dismiss my case. The judge ruled that he would "consider" reinstating the case only if Stefani brought me in to personally appear before him.

Stefani tried to explain to the judge that it would present a hardship for me to return to Michigan prior to trial, because I had to care for three small children. He also offered to produce a sworn affidavit from me attesting to the fact that I wanted my case reinstated.

The judge responded by saying that he didn't care where I was and that I must appear before him. Only then would he "consider" reinstating the case. The Honorable Warfield Moore, Jr. of the Third Judicial Circuit of Michigan denied the motion and abruptly invited Mr. Stefani to appeal his ruling.

On June 2, 2005, Stefani filed on my behalf a claim of appeal of right with the Michigan Court of Appeals with respect to the judge's order of dismissal and refusal to reinstate the lawsuit. I drove to

Detroit and met Stefani outside the Michigan Court of Appeals building.

I was a bit nervous and continuously stayed aware of my surroundings. I remained alert to any vehicle following or passing me on the road. When Mr. Stefani asked if I wanted to meet him at his office and ride down together, I declined. I figured if anyone wanted to harm or stop us, it would be too easy for them if we were in the same vehicle. Once I checked my weapon with security, we proceeded to the assigned court room.

I took a seat in the crowded courtroom and observed my attorney gallantly argue the reinstatement of my lawsuit. During the argument, he asked me to stand and explain to the judges that I was present and desired to have my lawsuit reinstated.

After Stefani closed his argument and we left the building, he expressed confidence that my lawsuit would be reinstated. I truly believed him; however, I was still recovering from his missing the settlement hearing. I wondered if he had gambled; he was too intelligent to lose.

When I returned to my car, I was apprehensive about entering it. I used my training and completed a thorough check for a car bomb. I then left Detroit as quickly as possible. I never wanted Stefani to know that I was afraid during any of our meetings.

On November 17, 2006, the Court of Appeals issued an unpublished opinion, Harris *v.* Jerry A. Oliver, Sr., and reversed the judge's dismissal of the lawsuit. In that opinion, the Court of Appeals ruled that the judge abused his discretion, because he was not authorized under MCR 2.401 and 2.504(B) to dismiss my lawsuit *sua sponte.* The Court of Appeals also ruled that he abused his discretion by failing to consider any options other than dismissal of my lawsuit.

The jurisprudence of Michigan courts is that dismissal for a plaintiff or a default judgment against a defendant is an extreme sanction that should be reserved only for the most egregious violations of the court rules. Before imposing such a sanction, the trial court is required to "carefully evaluate all available options on the record and conclude that the sanction of dismissal is just and proper" (*Brenner v. Kolk,* Mich 226 App 149, 163:573 NW2d 65 (1977). Fortunately, this presumed gamble or planned tactic worked in my favor. Mr. Stefani was able to reinstate my case which caused it to appear in court after the Nelthrope-Brown case.

# PART 4

# *The Aftermath*

# Chapter 15

# The Jury Verdict & Settlement

"Oaths are but words, and words but wind."
*Samuel Butler*

In August 2007, the 15-day trial of Brown and Nelthrope versus the City of Detroit began. I was called to testify in court. I took the time off from work at the Bloomington Police Department and drove to Detroit. My plans were to stay in a hotel outside the city limits under someone else's name. After talking to Nelthrope, he convinced me to stay at his apartment in the suburbs. He advised that it would be more convenient if we both rode together to the trial in the morning.

The night before the trial, I did not sleep a wink. I was worried that someone would either fire bomb the apartment or spray it with an AK-47. I lay in bed fully clothed and armed, anticipating I would have to jump out of the upstairs window to safety.

During our drive into the city for the trial, I kept my head on a swivel, anticipating trouble. I figured if the enemy decided to attack, two guns were better than one. Once downtown, we entered the Coleman A. Young Municipal Center, the location of the mayor's office where I used to work. I didn't like the fact that we had to check our weapons with the deputy sheriff prior to going to the courtroom. I really felt vulnerable the whole time, before and after I testified.

My testimony before the mayor and Christine Beatty lasted two days. I told about the various incidents that I had witnessed while working for Kilpatrick. I was asked about my relationship with Officer Nelthrope and some of the things that Jackson and Lewis had done in the unit. It seemed as though most of the questions asked of me were about Christine and other women. The questions primarily focused on the mayor's philandering ways.

During my testimony in the Nelthrope and Brown case, I wasn't asked about the harassment and intimidation I experienced. I believe that was reserved for my trial. I wasn't asked about my knowledge of the texting between the mayor and Christine, either. However, I was asked why I resigned from the department and moved out of state. I testified that I felt my family and I were in great danger. I did not exaggerate or embellish. I wish that I had had a chance to tell all that I went through, but the questions were limited to facts surrounding Brown and Nelthrope's case.

The psychiatrist, Dr. Rainey, testified that Nelthrope was exaggerating his claims of stress in asking for a duty-related disability. I'm sure if given the chance he would have said the same about me. Yet, I know without a shadow of doubt, my stress, agony, and torment were not imagined, exaggerated, or fictitious.

On August 28, 2007, Christine Beatty took the stand. Mr. Stefani asked her, "During the time period of 2001 to 2003, were you and Mayor Kilpatrick either romantically or intimately involved with each other?" Rolling her eyes, Beatty answered with an emphatic, "No." She was also asked if she took part in firing Gary Brown, to which she replied, "No."

Kilpatrick testified for more than three hours the next day. Stefani asked him, "Mayor Kilpatrick, during 2002 to 2003, were you romantically involved with Christine Beatty?" Kilpatrick's response: "No." During Kilpatrick's testimony, he answered to the speculation that he and Christine were lovers. "I think it was pretty demoralizing to her—you have to know her—but it's demoralizing to me as well. My mother is a congresswoman. There have always been strong women around me. My aunt is a state legislator. I think it's absurd to assert that every woman that works with a man is a whore. I think it's disrespectful not just to Christine Beatty but to women who do a professional job every single day. And it's also disrespectful to their families, as well."

With this lengthy retort it seemed to give more credence to how strongly he felt about the need to defend Christine's reputation. It also seemed to put him in a position where the jurors might see this as more than a business relationship.

The court case was based on the wrongful firing of Gary Brown and the exposing of Officer Nelthrope as a whistleblower. The jury was excused to deliberate on the possibility that Christine and the mayor conspired to fire Brown. After three hours of deliberation, the jury came back with a guilty verdict.

The jury found in favor of Brown and Nelthrope and awarded them $6.5 million, divided as $3.9 million for Brown and $2.6 million for Nelthrope. Mayor Kilpatrick vowed to appeal.

I watched the trial play out on my computer. I saw how angry and adamant the mayor was when he said he would fight the verdict in appeals. At this point I was very happy to hear the guilty verdict but knew that it wasn't over because an appeal can go on for years.

One afternoon while I was sitting in my apartment in Bloomington, I received a telephone call from Mr. Stefani. He explained that Mayor Kilpatrick agreed to pay a settlement for Brown and Nelthrope. Stefani did not go into detail on how much Brown and Nelthrope would receive. He then said my settlement would be $400,000, excluding any taxes taken before disbursement.

I immediately sat completely still and thought, FINALLY! Is this really happening? Stefani instructed me to sign the settlement agreement that would arrive the following day, open a bank account, and then contact him with the account number for wire transfer of the settlement funds.

I went straight to the bank and opened a savings account with $5.00 with the anticipation of receiving the settlement money. I called Nelthrope on my cell while driving home, and he was in the process of opening his savings account at the bank. I rushed home and called Stefani with the bank account number. He again reminded me to sign the settlement agreement and mail it back immediately.

I was so happy I had to call my wife at work! I told her I needed her to come home as soon as possible. Of course, she must have thought something was wrong with one of the kids. I reassured her that they were fine, but we needed to talk. I wanted to surprise her with the good news. She rushed home in a panic.

I told her to sit on the couch. She looked at me, did as I asked, and then waited to hear what I had to say next. Then I gave a great big smile and told her that Stefani had called me. She relaxed a bit and gave me a long "Okay?" I shared with her that the city had settled my case and that I had just opened an account for a big deposit coming in the next day.

She immediately jumped up and hugged me so hard. She started to cry in relief that our ordeal was finally over. She then sat down and became silent for a moment. I asked her if she was alright. "I feel sick to my stomach," she said. I think she was shocked, happy, and relieved all at the same time; it must have been a bit overwhelming. Needless to say, we later went out to our favorite restaurant for dinner with the kids to celebrate!

The next day there was a knock on the door. When I answered the door, the postman handed me a large envelope and instructed me to sign for it. The envelope contained a letter addressed to me stating the agreement should remain confidential and the terms should not be revealed to any person. The agreement stated that I could never mention the text messages to anyone or ask for my job back, after the settlement. The letter threatened that if I violated the agreement, I would forfeit the settlement and the legal fees. I really did not agree with the settlement, but I was advised that everyone needed to sign off to get paid. I knew if I didn't sign the document, I would hold up everyone else's money.

Although I was happy to hear that the city was willing to settle my case, I was surprised to learn of the "gag order" and the terms. Most of it concerned talking about the text messages. I thought it strange that I could never mention the text messages to anyone. I never had read the actual text messages. I just knew that they were texting each other during my assignment with the mayor's EPU. As for wanting my job back, I felt that I was a marked man and going back to work in Detroit wasn't an option for me.

The biggest surprise was the amount of my share of the settlement. I paused briefly to reflect on all that my family had lost financially: the rental property to foreclosure, our home, most of our personal possessions, and good credit rating. We had been forced into a financial hole. We were basically living paycheck to paycheck but still found ways to make our lives happy. The influx of this settlement money would allow me to pay off a lot of old debts. I was excited and knew that one day I could purchase my family a home again and start life all over. From the beginning of this lawsuit, however, it was never about the money. I wanted to clear my name and set the record straight!

I signed the document but before I could leave home to mail it, I received a call from Mr. Stefani. He asked if I had received the document, and then he quickly advised me to destroy it; another one was on the way. I was a little confused, but I followed his directive.

The following day I received a revised settlement agreement letter that was quite different. The words "text messages" had been removed, along with words, "I could not request my job back." The revised letter also stated that "the agreement shall remain confidential and its terms shall not be revealed to any person." I signed the document and mailed it to Stefani via express mail for next-day delivery.

I noticed that the settlement seemed to focus on my knowledge of text messages. I recalled that, prior to the start of the trial, Mr.

Stefani had subpoenaed SkyTel, the company managing the city's SkyPager® units. He wanted copies of the text messages. The judge hearing the case mandated that, once produced, those messages were to go to him for review of admissibility. To the best of my knowledge the messages were not received by the time the trial started. Certainly, Stefani gave me no indication that he was in possession of them.

Apparently, after the trial was over and the mayor vowed to appeal, I believe that Mr. Stefani subpoenaed again to receive the transcripts of text messages sent by Kilpatrick and Beatty. When I found out that the city decided not appeal the Brown and Nelthrope case and my case was added in a part of this settlement, I wondered if their decision stemmed from evidence found in the text messages. There certainly was reason to believe so, since there was wording in my settlement to not disclose information about them. I think the mayor's lawyers wanted to settle the lawsuit and keep the conditions of the settlement from the public.

On December 11, 2007, I received a call from Mr. Stefani. He said that the settlement funds had been transferred to my bank account the previous day. I thanked him for taking on my case and for helping me when no one else would.

"Everything you told me was the truth," he said.

I happily drove to the bank to check my account. I walked up to the teller and requested a balance. When I received my balance, I began screaming for joy on the inside. I went back to my car and sat quietly, thanking God for the outcome of the whistleblower ordeal. It was finally over! The settlement money was not a surplus of cash, as one would suppose, nor was it the full $400,000. Nonetheless, after all of the deductions, including taxes, I knew that the worst was behind us. We had a significant amount of accumulated debt to pay off. Ultimately I knew that we could slowly but surely put our lives back together financially and replace what we had lost in leaving Detroit.

Even though we were happy in Bloomington, my wife and I were not happy about raising our kids in a small apartment. We could not sell our home in Detroit and suffered that financial loss. It became embarrassing for both of us at times when people would ask, "When are you guys going to get a house?" Now I knew I could tell my wife that we would someday have a house again.

The settlement most certainly came at time when I was feeling frustrated about police work. In the spring of 2007, I had answered a shots-fired call on the east side of the city. I approached the area alone while waiting for back up. I was walking through an apartment complex and unexpectedly, a gunshot whizzed past me from 10 feet away. I was able to apprehend the subject and arrested him. From his jail cell, he began to initiate threats against me. In fact, he was caught on tape talking to his girlfriend and trying to develop a plan of action against me. The Indiana State Police investigated the threat. It turned out to be legitimate. I felt like lightning had struck twice!

By December 2007, I had been on a stress leave from the department for at least eight weeks. Working for a smaller department did not provide the support I felt I needed during this new situation. In other words, I didn't have the option of a desk-duty position while the threats were being investigated.

I continued to follow the news coming out of Detroit on my home computer. There was a lot of media buzz covering the "secret deal" between the mayor's lawyer and Mr. Stefani. Apparently, Stefani had reason to believe the mayor and Beatty had committed perjury. They lied about not firing Gary Brown and about not having an intimate relationship. Part of this agreement was to keep the text messages between the mayor and his mistress out of public record as part of the Brown-Nelthrope court case and settlement of my lawsuit.

I was surprised to read on the Detroit Free Press website in January 2008 that the newspaper had received copies of text messages between the mayor and Beatty. This was the first time that I was able to read exactly what the two had texted. I have no idea how the newspaper received the copies, and they did divulge their source. Ultimately, it showed how the mayor and Beatty did, in fact, have an intimate relationship. The texts were explicit and were clearly sent to and from each other. The texts also showed how Beatty gave misleading testimony about actually firing Gary Brown.

My eyes were glued to my computer screen! I couldn't believe the amount of detail they texted! For example:

**Christine Beatty -05/01/03** —"I was really kind of trippin' after that because of 2 reasons. I can't see living this way with us being a "secret" forever. I love you so much and I want to tell somebody, someday. (Smile)"

**Kwame Kilpatrick -05/08/03-**"yes ma'am. I want to touch you. Hug, hold, kiss, etc. What's up?"

I continued to read the article online where it said that "the text traffic appears to lend credence to allegations made by Harris, a former mayoral bodyguard, who filed his own Whistleblower suit." As I continued to read, the article talked about the Washington trip in 2002 where I testified that I saw the mayor and Beatty in a compromising position in the mayor's hotel room. My jaw dropped when I read:

"So we are officially busted! Damn that," Kilpatrick responded. "Never busted. Busted is what you see!"

That was texted during the Washington trip. Kilpatrick later told reporters that I had made up stories to get money from the city. He basically called me a liar on television. He even stood on the steps of the Manoogian Mansion and spoke of his devotion to family and God amid a media frenzy.

I thought that it was ironic how the mayor would proclaim his loyalty to God and family and then turn around and text his love to Christine Beatty. The article reported that on October 3, 2002 the mayor texted Beatty, "I'm madly in love with you."

"I hope you feel that way for a long time," Beatty answered. "In case you haven't noticed, I am madly in love with you."

I then reflected on the court trial when both of them were specifically asked by Mr. Stefani if they had had an intimate relationship, and they both responded, "No." That's when I realized that the exposure of these texts made them subject to perjury charges, a felony.

## Chapter 16

# The "Final" Chapter

"The truth is powerful and it prevails."
*Sojourner Truth*

Many things happened by the spring of 2008. First I was granted a retirement by the Bloomington Police Department. My law enforcement career was done! We even ended our search for a house in Bloomington because of the new threats. We felt like it was time to leave Bloomington and move to a larger city. We didn't make any immediate plans to move, but we were giving it much consideration. This time our move had to be well-planned. We ultimately left Bloomington later in the year when my wife found a new job.

ॐ    ॐ

Next, on March 24, 2008, Wayne County Prosecutor Kym L. Worthy formally charged Mayor Kilpatrick with eight felony counts. Christine Beatty was charged with seven felony counts. The counts included perjury, conspiracy, obstruction of justice, and misconduct in office. The prosecutor stood in the courthouse in front of the

American flag while delivering her press conference. She went on to say that she had zero tolerance for deliberate obstruction of justice.

Up to that point, the prosecutor's office, the local newspapers, and the Detroit City Council had been trying to retrieve the "secret" confidentiality documents from the city. The city attorneys were fighting it and the further release of text messages claiming that they were private and not subject to public disclosure.

That seemed to infuriate Prosecutor Worthy. During her press conference she stated, "At every bend and turn, there have been attempts by the city through one lawyer or another to block aspects of our investigation. We had to file motions to compel the release of documents. We had to appear in circuit court, respond in the Court of Appeals, and just last Friday we had to file paperwork in the Michigan Supreme Court to get them." She also talked about how the mayor's attempt to hide his relationship with Christine Beatty affected so many. I appreciated most what she said next:

> Let me be very, very clear this was not an investigation focused on lying about sex. Gary Brown, Harold Nelthrope, and Walter Harris, their lives were forever changed. They were ruined financially and their reputations were completely destroyed, because they chose to be dutiful police officers. The public trust was violated.

I sat at my computer at home and watched Prosecutor Worthy's press conference. I was somewhat anxious and excited, but I also felt vindicated. I also wondered if any law enforcement agencies with integrity were left in Detroit. It was unbelievable to see with my own eyes that justice finally was being served. I truly believed that Kwame

Kilpatrick was untouchable. I was and still am very proud of Prosecutor Worthy for having the intestinal fortitude to bring Kilpatrick and Beatty to justice.

I truly felt sad for Kilpatrick and Beatty too, along with their families. This dynamic duo could have been great for Detroit. I really don't hate them, just the evil acts they committed against me and others. Prosecutor Kym Worthy is a truth fighter and my hero.

> "Never explain, your friends do not need it and
> enemies will not believe it anyway."
> *Elbert Hubbard*

I have spoken to reporters, radio talk show hosts, and former co-workers; they all wanted to know after the settlement if I was angry that I didn't receive as much money as Brown and Nelthrope received. Did I feel that Michael Stefani had given me the shaft? Was I just an afterthought to force the city to settle my case? Did I realize that my testimony was the most damaging to Mayor Kilpatrick? Did I realize that my family suffered just as much as Brown and Nelthrope's families? The above questions were never asked by my friends but by outsiders.

I have always answered the questions the same: it was never about the money. It was about providing the truth and maintaining loyalty to my badge, not to a person or an administration. The badge is a symbol of my office, and I promised myself to never compromise it for anyone.

The thorns that Mayor Kilpatrick and Christine Beatty reaped are from the trees they planted. Officer Nelthrope was not only a fellow officer but a friend who was doing what every law enforcement officer should have done. He exposed corruption, and I corroborated his story. I believed that the system of justice would work; however I was terribly misguided. I was labeled as a rat by some officers on the police department and found dead rats on my doorsteps.

I imagined they wanted to know why I would speak out against the man I shared secrets with and swore to protect. I will always remember what my oldest brother, a law enforcement officer, shared with me before I became a police officer. He told me to honor the badge and not to compromise my integrity for anything or anyone. "Once you lie and are caught, you are no longer any good to the community, the police department, or the courts."

I simply provided the truth to the state police, to the attorney general, and to the media. I just wanted the opportunity to tell a jury what I knew and let them hear about the turmoil I experienced for blowing the whistle. When I returned to the precinct, I believe Kilpatrick did everything in his power to ruin my career. It was just disheartening to discover that the cavalry (police department administration) did not arrive to support or save me. In retrospect, people and agencies trembled at the power of Mayor Kilpatrick and his administration. I am forever indebted to Michael Stefani, and the law firm of Stefani and Stefani for their courage to take on Kilpatrick and his administration on my behalf.

When I reflect on the whistleblower ordeal, I think about the barrage of corruption that was uncovered. As a result of the whistleblower lawsuits by Brown, Nelthrope, and me, the entire administration for the City of Detroit has been altered. I believe it is for the betterment of Detroit citizens.

As a result of the text messages exposing the perjury of the mayor and Beatty, the Detroit City Council voted for Kilpatrick to resign. Christine Beatty also pled guilty to two felonies and served a four-month sentence.

"He is a classic American tragedy."
*Colin Hubbell*

On September 4, 2008, Mayor Kilpatrick pled guilty to two felony counts of obstruction of justice. As a result of his plea agreement, he had to step down as mayor, serve four months in the Wayne County Jail, and pay a million dollars in restitution to the City of Detroit. In addition, he was placed on five-year probation and could not run for public office. Sadly, he had to give up his license to practice law. On October 28, 2008, Kilpatrick began his four-month sentence. He was released after 99 days for time served.

Upon Kilpatrick's release, Compuware's CEO Peter Karmanos hired him to work for Covisint, an affiliate of the Detroit-based Compuware. He subsequently moved to Texas. The city put him on a payment plan of $6,000 a month. His lawyer later argued that Kilpatrick could pay only $6.00 per month, and Kilpatrick was able to reduce his payments to $3,000 a month. Alas, in May 2010, he was sentenced to serve 18 months in federal prison in Michigan for probation violations which included failure to pay the required amount of restitution.

# Chapter 17

# To Blow the Whistle or Not

The consequences to blowing the whistle can be extensive. There can be financial losses as well as loss of relationships and diminished mental health. However, to see wrong and not report it, in my opinion, makes the observer complicit. A law enforcement officer should consider many things before blowing the whistle on corruption, crime, behavior unbecoming of an officer, or any other wrongdoing. Although these considerations are specific to law enforcement, I believe that they can apply to anyone in any private sector workforce.

**Motives**
The first step should be to consider your motives. In my case, my motives were clearly to stand for what was right and to demand justice. In the process I was able to speak up and protect a co-worker who had become a friend. I believe that one's motive should never be about monetary gain. Don't become a whistleblower if all you want from it is to get paid. There are better ways to reap financial rewards by proper and legal means.

Some people may be motivated to blow the whistle for emotional reasons. Emotions can cloud your judgment and the facts. It is better to undertake such a task when the primary motive is to reveal an injustice, a criminal act, a violation, or something unethical and/or immoral.

## Options

You should consider your options once you have decided that you must report a wrongdoing. The options should be clear to you. Unfortunately, my options were limited. I believe that everything I witnessed was a significant violation worthy of reporting. In hindsight, I think maybe I should have gone directly to Internal Affairs, but I saw that Brown already had been fired and felt that the confidentiality of that department had been compromised. I saw my friend Nelthrope on television exposed as "The Whistleblower" and then called a liar by the mayor. I knew what Nelthrope reported was true, because I had witnessed most of it first-hand. I was shocked that he did it but once it was public, I felt compelled to corroborate his report.

The media became my outlet as part of blowing the whistle. I was also able to use the inquisition of the Michigan State Police as an opportunity to divulge things that I had witnessed. Using the media wasn't planned; it just happened. As Nelthrope's crew leader, I was put into a position to either deny or confirm his statements.

On the spur of the moment, my life changed forever. I didn't have time to stop and think of the potential fallout of my support of Officer Nelthrope. When the media put me on the spot, my instinct was to tell the truth. Afterwards, I thought it would be okay, because the chief of police would be happy to step in and discipline Officers Lewis and Jackson. I thought the chief would later give me a pat on the back with an "atta boy, Walt, you did a good job disclosing the misconduct of these officers." Sadly, that wasn't the case. Instead, it all came back to me in the form of harassment. Therefore, I believe that if you make the decision to blow the whistle, choose your outlet wisely.

**Evidence**
I have heard this said in a movie, "It's not what you know, but what you can prove," and there is a lot of truth to this statement. Any whistleblower must consider his evidence as well as reputation if standing solely on his word. I had to stand on my word and reputation, and that is why I believe they tried to discredit me. I wish now that I had kept a written log or journal of the specific threats and acts of intimidation. My option was to confide in Nelthrope and one other close friend in the event something happened to me. I strongly recommend that you collect any and all evidence and store it in a safe place.

**Results**
The desired outcome for any whistleblower is to see the involved parties be held responsible for their misconduct or wrongdoing. Basically, it is to right a wrong and to believe that it will make a difference for people in the future. In the end, it should discourage employers, corporations, and people of power from carrying out wrongful acts.

In my case, Detroit's entire administration was reorganized. New people have come into the mayor's office and police department to try to establish a more positive regime and rebuild the city's reputation with integrity. It feels good to be vindicated and have your personal name and reputation restored. It is hard to look too far forward to answer the questions you may have: What are my chances? Will the outcome be successful? I had to take it one day at a time, follow through with the demands of the lawsuit, and wait patiently. Waiting patiently is the difficult part. Having faith that truth will prevail is my best advice.

## Support

Make sure you have a strong support system in place. Having a spiritual leader, pastor, or minister that you can turn to for guidance will help. I found it most helpful to have at least two close friends to confide in, someone to talk to at any time of day, and someone who listened without being judgmental.

Initially, I didn't tell my wife what I was going through in the EPU; I only told her that I wanted out sooner than later. She was pregnant with our third child during the majority of the time that I worked for Kilpatrick. It was a difficult pregnancy, and she spent the last few months on bed rest. I didn't want to scare her when the harassment started. I think that you cannot "dump" this type of fear on your spouse and assume it won't affect them, scare them, or cause some mental anguish. You should share with them as much as you think they can handle. In the long run, it will all come out. In order to maintain a good relationship with your spouse or significant other, the sooner you tell them the better. It will give them time to adjust to the changes you are going through and how it has affected your relationship.

Basically, once you start a whistleblower action, you should be prepared that your family will go through it with you. Eventually, I had to inform my wife of everything and was grateful to finally tell her what was going on. Of course, she knew something wasn't just "right" when I left the EPU and returned to the precinct. She sensed a change in me, and it was only fair to her to finally tell her what was happening to me. After many long talks, we knew the best thing to do was to uproot our family and move out of state for our safety and peace of mind.

In the end, make sure that you and your family have the resolve and stamina to endure a court case that could last for years. Be sure you can endure the financial hardships that might follow and the potential loss of friends. Ask yourself, "What is the worst thing that can happen? Can you live with the worst to get to the best?"

The worse for me was the loss of a career that I wanted to last for many, many years. My childhood dream was to become a Detroit police officer. My college major was criminal justice, and I thought I could have a long-term career with the department.

The end result of blowing the whistle may not result in a lawsuit. However, if it does, you need to know that you might lose your trade or profession. Don't look for the end result to give you financial gain. Many will and have, yet I believe that no matter what you lose, you will gain more in the satisfaction of knowing that you did the right thing. I can look at myself every day in the mirror with dignity, self-respect, and no regrets.

# Appendix

# Things You Should Consider Before Blowing The Whistle (Checklist)

**What is my motive?**

(a) Was the improper conduct criminal, ethical, or immoral?

(b) Is this a revenge factor because I feel disrespected or am I acting on my emotions?

(c) Did I make a choice to stand for what is right and demand justice?

(d) Am I speaking up to protect a friend, co-worker, or myself?

**What are my options?**

(a) Should I try to report the violation anonymously?

(b) Did I address the violation through the proper channels?

(c) Am I protected under the Whistleblower Protection Act?

**Can I provide evidence? "It's not what you know, but what you can prove."**

(a) Did I keep a daily journal with good notes?

(b) Did I collect any evidence and store it in a safe location?

(c) Was the evidence collected lawfully?

(d) Will the evidence collected prove my case?

(e) Can I share the evidence with a trustworthy person in the event something happens to me?

**Desired outcome for the whistleblower**

(a) To hold involved parties responsible for their misdeeds

(b) To discourage future wrongful acts by the employer or employee

(c) To be vindicated for exposing wrongdoing

**Do I have a support system in place?**

(a) Do I have a spiritual leader, pastor, or minister to counsel me?

(b) Is there at least one close friend I can confide in or talk to at anytime of the day?

(c) Is there someone I can talk to who won't judge me?

(d) Do I have the necessary funds to support an out-of-state move or unemployment for a period of time?

(e) Do I have a physician to consult about anxiety and depression?

(f) Is there a facility or gym where I can work out daily?

(g) Is there a former employer who knows my work ethic, where I left a job in good standing? Hopefully they may rehire me, if I resign or am fired.

**What could the ultimate price be for blowing the whistle?**

(a) How will reporting this violation effect my employment?

(b) Will I be blackballed in my trade or profession?

(c) Will I be alienated from co-workers and friends?

(d) Will I lose the support from friends and family because of the publicity?

(e) Am I prepared for the strain that will be placed on my family's finances, relationships, and mental state?

(f) Do my family and I have the resolve and stamina that can sustain a court case lasting over several years?

(g) Am I prepared for the various forms of harassment verbal and non-verbal that might result from my blowing the whistle?

(h) Am I prepared to move out of state?

(i) What is the worst thing that can happen? Can I live with the worst to get to the best?

CPSIA information can be obtained at www.ICGtesting.com

260171BV00002B/61/P